HAUTE CUISINE

Haute Cuisine

HOW THE FRENCH INVENTED

THE CULINARY PROFESSION

Amy B. Trubek

PENN

UNIVERSITY OF PENNSYLVANIA PRESS   *Philadelphia*

Published by
University of Pennsylvania Press
Philadelphia, Pennsylvania 19104-4011

Library of Congress Cataloging-in-Publication Data
Trubek, Amy B.
    Haute cuisine : how the French invented the culinary profession / Amy B. Trubek.
        p.   cm.
    Includes bibliographical references and index.
    ISBN 0-8122-3553-3 (alk. paper)
        1. Cookery, French—History.   2. Gastronomy—History.   I. Title.
TX719 .T78   2000
641.5944'09—dc21   00-023286

CONTENTS

ILLUSTRATIONS

Your first great restaurant meal is a rite of passage. The stuff of countless stories over other dinner tables after several bottles of wine, you describe the moment when you realized that eating this meal was a transformative experience. During that magical meal, you were lifted above the everyday concern for nourishment into a domain of sensual pleasure. My moment of epiphany came at Le Français, a bastion of French haute cuisine hidden away in a suburb of Chicago. It was the summer of 1983, and I had just turned twenty. Throughout high school and college I had been an avid cook, and over the years I had worked in local restaurants and for catering companies. I somehow convinced my parents to take me, my sister, and a family friend to dinner at Le Français, over two hours from our home. The chef-owner is Jean Banchet, originally from Roanne, France. Winner of nine consecutive Mobil Travel awards, his restaurant is considered one of the premier fine dining establishments in the United States.

The evening was unforgettable. Years later I can still remember entering the restaurant, eyes ever widening as I absorbed the beautiful copper pots hanging from the walls, the plush banquettes, and the seemingly endless array of waiters. We were seated at a big round table in a corner, as if in a private dining room. With time, some details of the meal have faded, but in my mind's eye I still see the magnificent dessert, a mille-feuille with fresh raspberries and blackberries, surrounded by a pool of crème anglaise and drizzled with a caramel sauce. With the attentive service, the elegant setting, and the glorious food, I felt ennobled and enriched. As we left the building, I knew this was a world I must explore.

As I journeyed further into the world of fine dining, I realized that Le Français was but one restaurant among many run by Frenchmen and serving French haute cuisine. When I decided to cook in restaurants, the association between France and fine dining became even more dramatic. The domination of the French began to puzzle me, even haunt me. I realized that my initial rite of passage truly was a journey to a foreign land when I first stepped into a professional kitchen as an apprentice at the Peacock, a small fine dining restaurant in Cambridge, Massachusetts, after I graduated from college. There I learned how to julienne carrots, how to make liver pâté, how to coat a fillet of sole with a beurre blanc. My fascination with the influence of the French persisted when I went to the Cordon Bleu school in London and learned methods and techniques of French classic cuisine. Each morning we prepared a menu, comprised of such dishes as oeufs pochés cressonnière, côtes d'agneau farci, and pommes dauphinoise, which we ate for lunch. Most memorable was the day I prepared poulet farci parisienne. I boned the chicken, stuffed it with a forcemeat of ham and veal, and then sewed, trussed, and roasted it. For presentation as part of a grand buffet, I coated the chicken with a white chaudfroid, decorated it with flowers made of vegetables, and covered the entire piece with aspic. As I carefully spooned the clear gelatin over the now practically unrecognizable chicken, I wondered why I needed to master *this* to get my advanced certificate.

I went on to graduate school to learn more about the culture and history of food, particularly in the public sphere. Eventually I wanted to travel farther than France, and so I initiated research on cuisine in India. As I interviewed chefs and caterers at hotels in southern India, however, France would not go away, and my questions concerning the power of French cuisine became more intellectually central. Nowhere did the seminal nature of the connection between France and professional cuisine become more apparent than in a five-star hotel in Madras, India, when "Chef" Sunder Singh showed me around his kitchen. Standing stiffly in his crisp white chef's jacket and pressed checked pants, toque on his head, the chef pointed to a work table and said: "This is where I do my mise-en-place." The French had traveled far indeed.

As it turned out, difficulties emerged when I chose to unravel the connection among France, French chefs, and contemporary fine dining. In Europe the medieval and contemporary periods have drawn a great deal of attention; scholars have not looked closely at the emergence of fine dining in the public sphere in the nineteenth century. Most have looked through the lens of cookbooks, especially the recipes, and with those have explored the cooking of the domestic sphere. Often missing were the voices of those who made the food, the men and women who labored every day to transform raw ingredients into sumptuous meals. Few, if any, have documented the history of cooks or chefs de cuisine: other than cookbooks and anecdotes, the past is mute. And great meals, unlike great buildings, leave few traces. One day, one decade, one century later, usually all that remains is a paper menu naming the courses. We don't know where the food came from, who cooked it, how the diners enjoyed their meal. Hotels, restaurants, and clubs rarely keep records about the people scurrying around in the basement of their buildings, sweating from the heat of stoves and ovens. To me, this excavation is merely the beginning, laying bare several important strata, so that other curious explorers may dig yet deeper.

There are two ways to read this book. The chapters tell the story of how the French "invented" the culinary profession. Or, while reading or after finishing the chapters, the reader can look at the Notes section. The first note in each section explains why certain approaches were taken, or how particular texts were considered, or where this book fits in the field of food studies or culinary history. These are for the student or scholar who wishes to understand more about one person's intervention into this exciting field of study, just beginning to put down roots and establish its identity.

INTRODUCTION

Wonderful fine dining establishments can be found in all the nations of Europe and North America, but everywhere the menus are dominated by the French. The method of preparation is French, as is the style of cooking, and the professionals are French (the majority of native-born French chefs presently work outside France). Girardet in Switzerland, Le Manoir aux Quatre Saisons in England, Lutèce, Le Français, Le Chanticleer, and Restaurant Daniel in the United States, to name a few, are destinations for gourmets. These restaurants, glowingly described in newspaper reviews and guidebooks as the temples of fine dining, are *of* France but not necessarily *in* France.

Furthermore, the French can be found in culinary schools, where future professional chefs are trained. In the first semester at a leading culinary school in the United States, students must master the fundamentals of stock preparation and learn the five mother sauces of French haute cuisine as well as their many derivations. In "Knife Skills" class they learn to hold the French chef's knife and perfect the transformation of raw vegetables into precise mirepoix, brunoise, julienne, and bâtonet. They also learn the biographies of French chefs Antonin Carême and Auguste Escoffier and are told to buy the *Larousse Gastronomique* and *Le Guide Culinaire*, early twentieth-century bibles of French haute cuisine. They must come to the kitchen each day in their white chef's jacket and pressed checked pants, cloth toque upon their heads, a uniform almost identical to that worn by French chefs in France during the nineteenth century. The culinary school Le Cordon Bleu, which currently has branches in London, Paris, and Osaka, states that "thousands of students are enrolled at the Cordon Bleu, all having come . . . for the same reasons: to work with French chefs and learn from their skills."[1]

French chefs founded the leading professional culinary association in twentieth-century America—the American Culinary Federation. With 25,000 members, the ACF has chapters in every state except North Dakota. The association provides the only comprehensive certification program for culinary professionals outside culinary schools; more than 8,400 certifications have been awarded for cooks, sous-chefs, executive chefs, master chefs, and culinary educators.

Founded in 1929, the American Culinary Federation was an attempt to bring together three existing culinary associations: the Société Culinaire Philanthropique, the Vatel Club, and the Executive Chefs de Cuisine of America. The leading figure in the move to consolidate was Charles Scotto, former president of the Executive Chefs de Cuisine and the Vatel Club and past vice president of the Société Culinaire. He became the first president of the American Culinary Federation. Born in Monte Carlo in 1886, Scotto apprenticed under French pâtissiers and trained in London under Auguste Escoffier, often called the greatest French chef of the modern period. Scotto came to the helm of the American culinary association with a perfect French pedigree.[2]

French chefs, whether working within the borders of France or far away, have their own professional association: Les Maître Cuisiniers de France. Founded in 1951, the organization has three hundred members, of whom fifty-one belong to the American chapter. Entry requirements are very stringent. You must be a native-born Frenchman and have been nominated by two other members of the organization. To be considered, you must have been an apprentice for at least three years under a master chef trained in classic French cuisine in the style of Auguste Escoffier. The organization's charter extols the tasks of a true master chef: "The Master chef of France must be aware that he belongs to a renowned cultural tradition," and "as an heir to a great past, his mission is to serve the culinary art by expanding its influence and providing for its future." Among the Maître Cuisiniers de France found in the United States are Georges Perrier of Le Bec-Fin, Daniel Boulud of Restaurant Daniel, Jean Joho of Everest, and Michel LeBorgne of the New England Culinary Institute.[3]

Why do French chefs dominate fine restaurant kitchens, as they have since the nineteenth century? Why do budding American chefs still read *Le Guide Culinaire*? Why do so many people think French cuisine is superior to all others? Above all, why is French cuisine so *powerful* in the world of fancy food? The simple answer is that French chefs have dominated as the masters of the practice and as the primary instructors in the culinary knowledge necessary in fine dining restaurants, hotels, and clubs since their very inception. The discourse and practice of the French, or what is said and what is done, have always provided the framework for action far beyond France: the French invented the cuisine of culinary professionals.

How best to explore the persistent power of France in the world of fancy restaurants, hotels, and clubs? To unravel the puzzle, to understand the "reason why a particular structure of meaning [and practice] persists over time," we must turn to the past and perform a "genealogy of the present."[4] Because France dominates, the initial journey needs to be there, through the historical development of a *haute cuisine*, the type of food always the province of chefs and the precursor of professional cuisine. The courtly homes of the medieval and early modern period housed the beginnings of a French haute cuisine. With the development of the public sphere and the advent of the French Revolution, food production and preparation were transformed, but a dedication to the initially noble haute cuisine continues. The historical connection between France and the emergence of professional cuisine—food that is consumed in restaurants, hotels, and clubs and is prepared by trained experts—begins with the type of food prepared.

Food preparation of any kind depends on locale and audience; haute cuisine has always been prepared for people with allegiance to each other. Haute cuisine in France first appears in the stately châteaus and manors of the French aristocracy. This is hardly a controversial statement, given that before the late 1700s homes were the only places where people could expect to sit down to be served a formal meal. Although prepared food was available for purchase as early as the 1300s, it was found at town markets or at roadside stands that served itinerant travelers and pilgrims. Only much later would people go inside a building to be served a meal. Large, elegant manors were the site of professional cuisine's precursor and the places where chefs were first employed to ply their craft, which consisted of complex preparations presented to the aristocratic consumer in elaborate, multiple-course feasts.

As the story of professional cuisine unfolds, the link between cuisine and social hierarchy becomes increasingly clear: the gastronome Brillat-Savarin's insight "Tell me what you eat and I will tell you who you are" remains true long past the Revolution. The food produced by chefs was French *haute* cuisine, the cookery of the elites. The food of the peasant or the town baker, though not completely unrelated, was never seen to incorporate or represent the food of the chef. The audience for such a complex cuisine was always small, wealthy, and socially powerful: haute cuisine equals professional cuisine.

To delineate the differences and similarities between a cuisine and a haute cuisine, anthropologist Sidney Mintz asserts that not every society has a cuisine, but a society must have a cuisine in order to have a haute cuisine. His argument for sequence—first food, then cuisine, then haute cuisine—is important and compelling because these terms are too often used interchangeably, which may erase differences in geography, epoch, and social rank.[5] The everyday manifestations of such practices are complex, but certain generalizations about form and content can be made. Haute cuisines always have some relationship to an elite population, the cooks who are employed to make their food, and the ingredients and methods of preparation used.

Mintz's distinction among food, cuisine, and haute cuisine provides a good framework for understanding the type of food prepared by chefs from the Middle Ages through the present. Beginning in the medieval period, this "haute" cuisine was characterized by tremendous attention to the appearance of food, particularly in the case of the courtly feast.[6] Even for the aristocracy these feasts were major events and required the efforts of many people. Held in the great hall, they included musical and dramatic entertainment along with a sumptuous feast. Food, the *mets* in French, was often presented in the service of a larger pageant or drama called the *entremets*, in which roast beasts would make an entrance on a tower or candied fruits would arrive hanging from silver trees.[7] As Stephen Mennell argues, the importance of feasts to members of medieval society was in their function as an important site of social display: these feasts "and many other smaller-scale events were not merely entertainments and celebrations—they were a means of asserting social rank and power."[8] Feasts, and the special, complicated cooking required to create them, were needed to maintain social standing.

Le Viandier of Taillevent is an excellent source of information about the medieval haute cuisine. Taillevent's *Viandier* remains one of the earliest recipe collections of this period; in fact, only three earlier works are known.[9] Initially a handwritten manuscript, the work is difficult to date, but it was available as early as 1392, and several subsequent versions were published during the 1400s. The author, Guillaume Tirel, or Taillevent, was a maître-queux (master cook, or what today would be called chef de cuisine) to Charles V and was involved in professional service to French nobility for more than fifty years. Written by a practicing chef, the book was probably intended for other cooks working for the nobility. The array of recipes for a wide variety of game, fish, and fowl, seasoned with plenty of spices, indicates meals that were served to a wealthy audience. Organizing the recipes according to ingredients and methods, the author assumes that the reader knows a fair amount about techniques.

Le Viandier is divided into sections on meats, including roasts and stews; entremets; "dishes for the infirm"; fish, including freshwater, "round sea," and "flat sea"; sauces; and "additional recipes." There have been various interpretations of the underlying order to the cooking methods; for example, Terence Scully suggests that medical principles influenced Taillevent's techniques. Scully points out that a noble household would have a resident doctor as well as a resident chef, and given the importance of humoral theories, they would have worked together to create appropriate foods for the household.[10] The primary objective appeared to concern keeping food warm and moist, especially meats, fowl, and fish.

As an early work of the emerging haute cuisine, *Le Viandier* has three notable themes: the extensive use of spices to flavor the food; the separate preparation of the meats, fowl, and fish from the sauces that accompany them; and the complex instructions for presentation. This recipe for civé de veau, or veal stew, easily reveals these themes:

> Roasted on a spit or on the grill, without overcooking, cut up into pieces and fried in grease with chopped onions; steep burnt toast in wine and beef broth or in pea purée, and boil your meat with this; then add ground ginger, cinnamon, cloves, grains of paradise, and saffron for colour, infused in verjuice and vinegar. It should be thick, there should be enough onions, the bread should be dark and sharp with vinegar, and it should be yellowish.[11]

The flavoring agents are many and diverse. Cinnamon, cloves, and saffron would add a musky, earthy flavor; the ginger and cinnamon would add some sweetness; the grains of paradise would provide heat; and finally, the vinegar and verjuice (made from unripened grapes) would have brought a sour note to the dish. The meat is roasted, added to a sauce, and then boiled, a technique probably influenced by humoral theories: boiling the meat after roasting would serve as an antidote to the drying effect of roasting. A later, classical version of this dish would sear the veal in a pan and use that pan (with all the meat juices) to make the sauce. The meat would be braised in the sauce over a low heat, never boiled. Medieval haute cuisine is often criticized for a hodgepodge approach to flavor, especially compared to the more refined combinations of modern haute cuisine. When one looks at present-day fine dining dishes, however, their combinations often appear markedly similar to those of Taillevent.

At feasts, large fowl such as swan and peacocks would often be presented whole with their skin and feathers sewn back on after the fowl had been roasted. Taillevent's recipe for "Cigne Resvestu, or An Entremets of Swan Redressed in its Skin with all its Plumage," which is quite short, but definitely not simple, goes as follows:

> Take the swan and inflate it between its shoulders as with *Stuffed Poultry* and slit it along its belly, then remove the skin together with the neck cut off at the shoulders, and with the legs remaining attached to the body; then fix it on a spit interlarded as with poultry, and glaze it; and when it is cooked, it should be redressed in its skin, with the neck either straight or flat; it should be eaten with yellow Pepper Sauce.[12]

Several centuries later, a reader of medieval texts did not approve: "Even in his [Richard II's] time we find French cooks were in fashion; and they appear to have equalled their descendants of the present day, in the variety of their condiments and their faculty of disguising nature, and metamorphosing simple food into complex and non-descript gallimaufries."[13]

Flavor and color were important considerations. Cooks were interested in making dishes bright in color, and they often dyed sauces and covered roasts with gold and silver leaf.[14] The visual impact of a dish was a significant component of fancy medieval food; many dishes were dyed bright colors with saffron, wine, or mulberries.[15] Flavor was derived primarily from the use of spices, which came almost exclusively from the Far East and were the luxury commodities of the day. The importance of spices to medieval haute cuisine cannot be underestimated: "Never before and never since were so many spices used in European cooking."[16] Among the most frequently used spices in French aristocratic households during the fourteenth and fifteenth centuries were sugar, ginger, cinnamon, pepper, saffron, cloves, galingale, grains of paradise, cubeb, mace, nutmeg, and long pepper.[17] Spices functioned as more than a flavoring agent; they were also part of the repertoire of the medieval apothecary. In medieval noble households, spices were so valuable and expensive they were kept in special locked cabinets, and evidence suggests that cooks would request or buy the spices from the apothecary.[18]

As early as the 1300s, spectacle and complexity characterize haute cuisine. And for hundreds of years the spectacles were held in aristocratic households and the complex dishes were created by chefs hired to work in their kitchens. However, though the form of the food remains very similar, the content begins to shift. By the seventeenth century, chefs working in aristocratic kitchens began to experiment with the look, taste, and feel of food. Although the type of guests at the banquets remained the same, the chefs began to move their craft in a new direction.

Such changes in culinary sensibility can be traced to an overall shift in European cultural values toward the notion of civility; social class was indicated by social refinement.[19] By 1651, La Varenne, considered a major figure in the move to such a new culinary sensibility, talks in the dedication of his cookbook *Le Cuisinier Français* of his education in "the secrets of preparing foods delicately."[20] In this book, preparations now considered basic to French haute cuisine—bouillon, liaisons, roux, farces—are provided.[21]

Almost a century later, the revision of haute cuisine to a more refined modern sensibility remained a preoccupation of many cookbook authors. In *Les Dons de Comus ou L'Art de la Cuisine*, first published in 1739, François Marin exhorts the reader to aim toward a more elegant style of preparation. The preface of the 1758 edition argues for a judicious use of spices: "Seasoning is the downfall of mediocre workers, and the part of our work that needs the most attention. Salt, pepper, and the other spices, are ingredients more precious than gold when they are used properly, but true poisons when used extravagantly."[22] In another passage, Marin speaks positively of the changes to the culinary art in recent times, for "cooking is no longer a lethal practice when the principles are well-known and when dealt with by an artist."[23]

When discussing the shift in culinary sensibility, Marin makes a distinction between *la cuisine ancienne* and *la cuisine moderne*. La cuisine ancienne was the culinary fashion created by the French and exported from France until the early 1700s. Cuisine moderne comes from the ancienne tradition, but is less complicated and uses more scientific principles. He also talks of the inherent frailty of the human body and how food should help preserve health and not induce suffering.[24] The body has become a temple and the tongue a sensitive organ.

In 1828, Antonin Carême wrote in a similar vein. His second edition of *Le Cuisinier Parisien, ou L'Art de la Cuisine Française au Dix-Neuvième Siècle* compares menus and recipes of the cuisine ancienne and the cuisine moderne to show the "vast superiority" of the cuisine moderne because of its "simplicity, elegance, and sumptuousness."[25] Carême was considered by many subsequent professional chefs to be a great culinary artist who began to simplify the vestiges of medieval pageantry in the courtly haute cuisine. His cookbook still contains elaborate galantines, drawings of various socles, or edible pedestals, along with basic recipes, however. Carême's recipe and designs for socles made of lard in *Le Cuisinier Parisien* are conceived according to a "completely modern taste," and he describes them to be "virile" and "elegant."[26] These edible pedestals, usually elaborately carved or decorated, were a vital part of the presentation of the dish and were placed in the middle of the table for all to see. His galantine of turkey rests on a socle carved with classical columns and botanical decorations and uses hâtelets (metal skewers) as a garnish, some skewered with truffles.

Resonances may be found between medieval and modern haute cuisines, as in the emphasis on providing for diners visually dramatic showpieces, from the stuffed peacock to the galantine of turkey on a carved pedestal made of lard. Despite the chefs' pronouncements of a culinary revolution, during both eras the preoccupation of haute cuisine remained the transformation of nature into culture. Take the pedestrian bird, the chicken or goose fresh from the barnyard, and stuff, mold, coat, and decorate it. Voilà, the lowly bird becomes a work of art. Thus, though the content of the cuisine underwent significant transformation, strategies for proving *hauteness* persisted.

The interest in the transformation of nature into culture continues over large sweeps of French history, but what changes as the eighteenth century shifts to the nineteenth are the locations where chefs ply their craft. By 1830, some chefs continue to cook in noble households, but more work in hotels, restaurants, and clubs. Many work not in France but in Britain, Italy, Germany, and the United States.

Thus the next link in the historical chain between France and professional cuisine can be found in the shift from the noble home to the public restaurant. The complex dishes of the haute cuisine become commodities, bought and sold in the commercial milieus of the European urban areas, cementing the move from patronage to market. The haute cuisine that emerged from France is unusual compared to, for example, the haute cuisines of China or India. There are three main reasons: consumption never remained exclusively within the French court and elite members, but rather extended to elites throughout Europe; the cuisine was rigorously codified with the development of two written genres, cookbooks and culinary journals and magazines; and by the nineteenth century, French haute cuisine had become identified with professional mastery throughout Europe as well as the United States.

Although France was its homeland, from the beginning professional cuisine depended on international patronage and sites across the globe to survive and flourish. The real geographical locale—the city of Paris, the Rhône Valley, the Mediterranean—slips behind the curtains at crucial times, for France is at times territory, at times symbol. Professional cuisine's historical nerve center may have been in France, but the tentacles spread far across national boundaries. To follow the story as it unfolds, we will move in and out of France.

"The customer always comes first" is the mantra of the contemporary food service industry. At first glance this is just another example of our contemporary consumer culture, but another look reveals the necessity of the diner to food consumed in the public sphere. Without someone willing to purchase a galantine of turkey resting on an elaborate edible pedestal, the chef has little reason to create it. The customer plays a primary role when French haute cuisine enters the public sphere; the benefits of patronage, especially the assurance of an audience, can no longer be assumed. Consumers provide the financial fuel that keeps a restaurant or hotel in business. They create the demand and thus must come first.

Looking at food in the public sphere requires a consideration, however, of the social position and class status of not just the diner but also the chef. In the complex world of fine dining after it entered the public sphere and became an established part of urban life, chefs played a vital role in determining the taste and shape of the food, as well as the symbolic significance of fine food as a marker of hauteness. In this new milieu, the chef can influence the customer and make him want the galantine, establishing the desire.

The categories of consumer, producer, and public sphere are considered in my quest to understand the persistent power of France in the world of fine dining after 1800. How did French influence emerge historically? What were the values, the connections, and the results of their interactions? This book generally proceeds chronologically, moving at times from as early as the eleventh century through the nineteenth and into the early twentieth century. The period from 1870 to 1910 receives the most attention, for this era has the greatest implications for understanding the present and thus offers the best strata for a genealogical excavation.

To tell the story of professional cuisine and explain the mystery and magic of contemporary fine dining, I examine food both as a cultural symbol and as a means for creating social distinction. However, the primary actors use food—as both commodity and symbol—in more complex ways than studies have traditionally suggested. The role of the worker cannot be underestimated. Beginning in the mid-nineteenth century, chefs made French haute cuisine more than a convenient sign of social status for European elites. Adopting the cuisine for their own social purposes, chefs made it a marker of their own status as elite culinary professionals. The world of feasts, banquets, and elegant dinners has never been the same.

I THE CUISINE

In 1750 the world of haute cuisine was similar to earlier eras: it was created in the homes of the aristocracy, bounded by their demands, and greatly influenced by the aesthetic values of the day. Changes occurred in the activities of chefs, however. The act of putting pen to paper was most significant. With the development of cookbooks, rather than notebooks of receipts or orally transmitted recipes, chefs began to articulate a theory of cooking as much or more than a manual for action, and haute cuisine became codified. This process did not begin until the late sixteenth century at the earliest. Some scholars see Casteau's *Ouverture de Cuisine* (1604) as the first book published in France that articulates a code. "One feels that the distance between the cook and the printed page has been greatly reduced and that the cook is in the habit of talking and even writing about his craft."[1] The "classic" version of French haute cuisine was in place by the 1650s. La Varenne's *Le Cuisinier Français* (1651) is most important, for his book combines an "integrated repertory of techniques, basic mixtures, and raw materials, governed by acceptable rules."[2] With his more systemic approach, La Varenne has been called "the founder of French classical cooking."[3] From the 1750s on, published cookbooks such as *Les Dons de Comus* and *Le Cuisinier Parisien* combine all the necessary components for a codified cuisine, and classic French haute cuisine defines expert knowledge more generally.

During the 1700s the recipe and the cookbook took on their now familiar characteristics, and tremendous continuity can be seen in the structure and content of cookbooks on French haute cuisine throughout the next 250 years. Above all, with the increased use of the written word to transmit culinary knowledge, the cuisine becomes less permeable to change. A recipe exists as part of a permanent record, rather than as part of an oral tradition passed along from chef to apprentice. Cookbooks transmit knowledge, and thus their content has tremendous significance to culinary practice. The principles articulated in the cookbooks on French haute cuisine published since 1750 are still taught as the building blocks of haute cuisine and have persisted through the present day as the core of the professional culinary discourse and practice.

With the increased interest in cookbooks and their wider use in culinary practice, chefs demonstrated to a much larger audience their mastery of the cuisine and became the true champions of culinary hauteness. Everyday cooking, born out of necessity, produced in the domestic sphere, overlaps but does not link directly with the haute culinary discourse. A tradition of cookbooks aimed toward the bourgeois housewife or her (usually female) domestic servant did arise, notably Menon's *La Cuisinière Bourgeoise* (1790), Audot's *Cuisinière de la Campagne et de la Ville* (1818) and Saint-Ange's *La Cuisine de Madame Saint-Ange* (1827). These books were intended to provide practical and accessible information about cooking to a primarily female audience. By the late 1800s, professional chefs also made forays into the domestic market, but their aims were quite different.

Jules Gouffé's classic *Le Livre de Cuisine*, first published in 1868, was divided into two sections, "La Cuisine de Ménage" (Household Cuisine) and "La Grande Cuisine." He explains his strategy in the preface: "These two branches [of cuisine] correspond, and without a doubt complement each other . . . but in reality they represent two different lines of work."[4] In the first section on "La Cuisine des Ménages,"[5] "Preliminary Reflections," he provides the concepts and basic principles that are the foundation, to him, of all cuisine, and says that they must be understood to attain any level of professional skill. His rhetorical stance consistently makes the distinction between professional and domestic cooking paramount, as seen in the assertion that "the task of the female bourgeois cook is not at all the same [as that] of the chef of a noble household."[6] The masters of French haute cuisine saw themselves as educators from the lofty heights of the haute cuisine. Ironically, given their sense of difference, many chefs published books and articles aimed at teaching French women the proper way to cook. A combination of elitism and missionary zeal characterize the attitude of male French chefs toward French women, as will be discussed later. In fact there are more male chefs than female cooks who are cookbook authors, which makes France unusual in the overall history of cookbook production.

The building blocks of classic French haute cuisine are the ingredients, techniques, and methods that emerged from the eighteenth-century noble homes of France. An examination of a variety of cookbooks published since 1750 reveals the longevity of this body of knowledge and practice. The following outline of "classic" French haute cuisine's foundational principles is not a complete representation of the cuisine, nor is its complexity justly served. This outline illustrates the historical level of commitment to its principles. Later on, classic French haute cuisine will be discussed with great passion by British consumers and French chefs.

One point needs to be clarified, however. French chefs have an interesting but at times confusing tendency to herald changes in haute culinary practices by calling the new cuisine "nouvelle," thus in effect renaming what was called "moderne" cuisine by its practitioners to "classique." By 1890 Carême's *la cuisine moderne* has become *la cuisine classique,* and by 1975 Escoffier's work has become *la cuisine classique* in light of the *nouvelle cuisine* of a new generation of chefs such as Fernand Point and his disciples, including Paul Bocuse, Pierre Troisgros, and Michel Guérard. For purposes of clarity, I will call all French haute cuisine after 1750 classical haute cuisine.

Components

The five fundamental components of classical French haute cuisine are stocks, sauces, knife skills, cooking methods, and pastry.

STOCKS

If one were to choose only one aspect of classical French haute cuisine as the foundation of the overall structure, it would be its use of stocks and sauces. What has always distinguished French cuisine from its European counterparts has been the way meats and fish are not simply roasted or grilled or fried, but also coated with a sauce or braised in a liquid. As Auguste Escoffier says in chapter 1 of *Le Guide Culinaire* (*The Escoffier Cookbook*): "Indeed, stock is everything in cooking, at least in French cooking. Without it, nothing can be done. If one's stock is good, what remains of the work is easy; if, on the other hand, it is bad or merely mediocre, it is quite hopeless to expect anything approaching a satisfactory result."[7] Fifty years later, Julia Child voices a similar attitude in *Mastering the Art of French Cooking*: "Sauces are the splendor and glory of French cooking. . . . A sauce should not be considered a disguise or a mask; its role is to point up, to prolong, or to complement the taste of

Figure 1. Julia Child demonstrating how to decorate a cold poached salmon with a chaudfroid sauce on her television show. Copyright Paul Child. Schlesinger Library, Radcliffe College.

the food it accompanies, or to contrast with it, or to give variety to its mode of presentation."[8]

Escoffier defined the classical principal fonds de cuisine, or foundation sauces and stocks, as follows:

1. Ordinary and clarified consommés.
2. Brown stock or "estouffade," game stocks, the bases of thickened gravies and of brown sauces.

3. White stock, bases of white sauces.
4. Fish stock.
5. The various essences of poultry, game, fish, etc., the complements of small sauces.
6. The various glazes: meat, game and poultry.
7. The basic sauces: espagnole, velouté, béchamel, tomato, and hollandaise.
8. The savory jellies or aspics of old-fashioned cooking.[9]

In this list it appears that consommé and stock are two completely separate preparations. In practice, however, consommé is simply stock (also called bouillon) that has been clarified of all impurities.[10] The decision to use stock or consommé depends on the final dish. Stock is used as a base for sauces, whereas consommé is used as a base for clear soups.

The importance of stock to French haute cuisine remains constant, though the proper method for preparing stock has undergone some changes. Escoffier's recipe for brown stock, or *estouffade*, uses beef bones, veal bones, raw ham, and fresh pork rind. The bones are browned in the oven and then put into a large stockpot with water, carrots, onions, and a bouquet garni (parsley, celery, thyme, and bay leaf). This mixture is simmered over a low fire for twelve hours. Finally, the ham and pork rind are cooked and added to the stock, and the liquid is strained.[11] Much of the method continues to be the same, though present-day stocks are made solely from one variety of meat: cooks make beef stock *or* veal stock. Pork is not used at all. The recipe for beef stock from one chef trained under several French chefs in the early 1980s includes beef bones, a mirepoix of vegetables (diced carrots, onions, and celery), and a sachet of parsley, thyme, bay leaf, and peppercorns. The proper method for stock preparation remains a subject of serious debate, and the quality of stock is used as a measure of competence among chefs. At a recent demonstration at the New England Culinary Institute, a visiting chef said, "And above all, when making a stock, *never* let the liquid come to a boil. Too many people try to rush a stock." Many of the culinary students nodded their head at this dictum; they had heard this many times. As a chef-instructor at the school said in cooking theory class, "The difference between someone I want to have in my kitchen and a shoemaker is in the attention paid to the stock." She then told the students her secret to a great stock: "All I can say is skim, skim, skim."

Since stock is considered vital to the quality of the more complex sauces and soups, which are the building blocks of the cuisine, French cookery books contain a myriad of suggestions on what is necessary to create the highest quality bouillon. In *Les Dons de Comus, ou L'Art de la Cuisine* (1739), the first chapter is devoted to bouillon, which the author calls "the soul of the cuisine."[12] Alexandre Dumas, in his *Dictionary of Cuisine* (1870), has this to say about bouillon: "Always take the biggest piece of meat practicable for your uses. The larger, the fresher, and the thicker the piece of meat, the more the bouillon will reflect these three good qualities, without counting the savings of time and fuel."[13] Chicken and veal stock (also known as white stock) and fish stock are made using the same principle of combining bones with vegetables and simmering them in water until their flavor essences permeate the liquid.

In the culinary literature, there appears to be a difference of opinion on the definition of essences. Escoffier states that they are "stocks which hold a large proportion of a substance's aroma in a concentrated form."[14] André Simon, in *A Concise Encyclopedia of Gastronomy,* defines essences more broadly: "In culinary French, essence means the natural juices of whatever has been cooked after such juices have lost by evaporation a large proportion of their moisture and reached the degree of concentration when their flavor is greatest and their bulk least."[15] Reduction of a cooking liquid, either stock or natural juices, over a high heat in order to concentrate its flavor is clearly an important technique in modern French cooking. Glazes, which are usually used to coat large pieces of meat, fowl, game, or fish, are the product of even more intensive reduction of liquid over a high heat, until the liquid reaches a glutinous consistency.[16]

During the mid-nineteenth century the aristocracy throughout Europe were entertaining each other with elaborate French dinners in which the sauce clearly reigned supreme. In 1867, in Italy, the prince de Carignan served a dinner for forty people that was typical of elite events featuring French haute cuisine. For the first course, the assembled guests dined on soupe tortue et consommé, or consommé of turtle, a clear broth made from fresh turtle meat that was an extremely popular dish of the time. In fact, the high demand for fresh turtle meat (which came primarily from the Caribbean) in the late nineteenth century decimated the native turtle population. Another dish served was quenelles à la Maintenon. Quenelles are molded balls of forcemeat, most often puréed seafood, that are poached in a simmering liquid until cooked. A Maintenon sauce uses as its base a soubise sauce, essentially an onion-flavored béchamel, but an egg yolk is added for extra richness, along with a julienne of tongue, ham, chicken breast, mushrooms, and truffles.[17] For the main fish course, guests ate saumon garni, with a sauce genevoise. *Le Répertoire de la Cuisine* defines a genevoise sauce to be a "mirepoix of vegetable and chopped salmon head, tossed in butter with mignonette pepper, thyme, bay leaves, faggot, moisten with red wine, reduce by half, add demi-glace and cook 40 minutes. Strained and finished with butter and anchovy essence."[18]

The meat course consisted of filet de boeuf à la jardinière, a truly classic example of French haute cuisine. Escoffier's recipe for this dish is as follows:

> Lard the filet and roast it.
>
> Set it on a meat platter and surround it with the following garnishes, which should be arranged in distinct heaps in such a way as to alternate their colors: Carrot and turnip balls done with a grooved ball cutter and cooked separately in consommé; peas, string beans cut in one inch pieces and small young kidney beans; each vegetable should be cooked in a manner in keeping with its nature, and separately mixed with butter; portions of freshly-cooked cauliflower, kept very white.
>
> Send some Hollandaise sauce for the cauliflower, and some clear gravy to the table, separately.[19]

To lard the filet, one takes long pieces of fatback, or lard dur, attaches them to a larding needle (aiguille à piquer for a small piece of meat, lardoire for a large piece of meat), and inserts the fat through the meat. Jacques Pépin demonstrated larding in his book La Technique, published in 1976. Once the rule for roasting meats, the practice was on the wane in the United States by the mid-1970s, probably because beef cattle were being fed more corn to make their meat naturally more fatty. Larding and barding are still done in France, however. Other than roasting the meat, the preparation for filet de boeuf à la jardinière involved elaborate presentations of minimally flavored vegetables.

Soups and sauces were essential for elaborate meals beyond the borders of France. In St. Petersburg, the Grand Duchess Hélène served twenty people a six-course meal, with fifteen dishes that included two soups, printanier à la française and purée de levraut à la Rossini. Also, trout was served with both hollandaise and genevoise sauces on the side.[20]

In our time at Le Cordon Bleu Cookery School in London, the first week of the basic cookery course, "Introduction to Classic Cuisine," is devoted to learning how to use a knife; the second and third weeks are devoted to learning about basic sauces, stocks, and soups. At Le Cordon Bleu in Paris, the third class, after the welcome and "Présentation et utilisation du matériel et des couteaux" (Presentation and techniques of equipment and knives), concerns les fonds de base (the basic sauces) and

discusses veal, chicken, and fish stock, béchamel sauce, and cheese souf-
flé. For years at the New England Culinary Institute, students were given
Le Répertoire de la Cuisine at registration. Originally published in 1914 and
promoted as a culinary dictionary, the small book by Louis Saulnier, a
disciple of Auguste Escoffier, lists in shorthand form recipes for all the
soups, sauces, roasts, and the like, of Escoffier's version of French haute
cuisine. Over seventy-five years after their initial publication, *Le Guide
Culinaire* and *Le Répertoire de la Cuisine* are still in print and are often used
as part of culinary education.

SAUCES

In addition to stocks, the repertoire of French haute cuisine contains a
multitude of sauces, in which different ingredients are added to stocks
and cooked in a number of ways. They all tend, however, to be variations
on the theme of several basic, or "mother" sauces: espagnole, velouté,
béchamel, tomato, and hollandaise.

The espagnole sauce is a combination of a dark roux and a meat stock.
A dark roux is made from flour and butter cooked over a medium heat to
make a thick paste for as long as it takes to allow the mixture to turn
brown in color. After the roux is incorporated into the liquid and simmered for a long period of time, chopped tomatoes are added. Velouté
and béchamel sauces also use roux as a thickening agent, but the flour-
butter mixture is not cooked as long as for the espagnole sauce, and
therefore retains a light color. Also, white or fish stocks are used for a
velouté sauce rather than the meat stock, and milk is used for a béchamel
sauce. Traditionally, these sauces, which are fairly thick in consistency,
have been used to coat a piece of fish or fowl or meat.

Another layer of complexity is added when one looks at what Escoffier labels "the small compound sauces."[21] He lists more than ninety
variations to the mother sauces in *Le Guide Culinaire*. Julia Child, in her
inimitable quest for democracy in the kitchen, has this to say about the
smaller sauces:

> While their roster is stupendous to look at, it is not mind-boggling
> when you begin to realize that their multitude divides itself into a
> half dozen very definite groups, and that each sauce in a particular
> group is made in the same general way. For instance, every sauce in
> the white sauce group of béchamels and veloutés calls for an identi-
> cal technique, but any change in ingredients or trimmings gives the
> sauce a new name: béchamel with grated cheese is a mornay, with

minced herbs, a chivry; while a white wine fish velouté with dollops of cream, egg yolk, and butter becomes an elegant sauce parisienne. Thus as soon as you have put into practice the basic formulas for a few mother sauces, you are equipped to command the whole towering edifice.[22]

Another set of sauces, egg based rather than stock based, are also important in French haute cuisine. The most classic is hollandaise sauce, in which butter is slowly incorporated into warmed egg yolks until the mixture reaches a creamy consistency. There are numerous variations to hollandaise sauce, including the popular béarnaise, which has the added ingredients of vinegar, shallots, and herbs, usually tarragon. Mayonnaise is a sauce based on the same egg-fat principle, but the eggs are cold and vinegar and oil are used. Again, as with the other sauces mentioned above, the French have developed numerous variations to the basic mayonnaise, including sauce rémoulade, which is mayonnaise with anchovies, pickles, capers, and herbs.

Finally, there is the category of savory gelatin and aspic. These "sauces" historically were extremely important in French haute cuisine, as Escoffier notes: "Aspic jellies are to cold cookery what consommés and stock are to hot. If anything, the former are perhaps more important, for a cold entrée—however perfect it may be in itself—is nothing without its accompanying jelly or aspic."[23] Extensive usage of aspic in cold dish preparation has waned during the course of the twentieth century. It is still considered an important piece of knowledge for a trained chef, however; Le Cordon Bleu continues to teach such classics as oeuf en gelée (egg in aspic). Aspic is made traditionally with calf's hooves or knuckles that are added to fresh stock and simmered; the natural gelatin in the animal bones should be enough to make the stock thicken and jell.

In today's French haute cuisine, one can see the importance of sauce to presentation as well as flavor. Much of the visual elegance of nouvelle and contemporary cuisine occurs with the unusual placement of the sauce on individual plates. This innovation resulted from the change in service that occurred with the rise of restaurants and hotels. Earlier forms of haute cuisine were either served to the diner as entire, elaborately decorated dishes or prepared as individual servings but displayed on platters, with the sauce brought out on the side. In the twentieth century, the attention shifted to the individual plate, and sauce became more central to the overall aesthetic of the food. A 1998 article on Frédy Girardet (until 1996 the chef-owner of a renowned Michelin three-star restaurant on Lake Geneva) showed him preparing warm salmon filets with fennel emulsion and provençal olive oil. The photograph displays the salmon filet surrounded by two concentric circles of sauce, one a fennel emulsion, the other a fish fumet; color is added to the disk with decorations of dill, green pepper, and tomato.[24]

KNIFE SKILLS

Also considered an important building block of French cuisine is a set of rules and techniques regarding the preparation of vegetables and fruits. Some of these rules and techniques are chiefly for purposes of presentation; others involve greater ease in preparation. At Le Cordon Bleu, on the first day of the basic cuisine class, students receive a written definition of the various important cuts of vegetables, for example, julienne, macédoine, and paysanne. There is a separate vocabulary for potato cuts—pommes mignonette, pommes château, pommes Pont-Neuf. In *Mastering the Art of French Cooking*, Julia Child devotes a special section to "Cutting: Chopping, Slicing, Dicing, and Mincing." Knowledge of these vegetable cuts is assumed in cookbooks on French cuisine from both the nineteenth and twentieth centuries: Felix Deliée's *Franco-American Cookery Book* includes recipes for potatoes à la Mantaise and salad à la macédoine,[25] and in Patricia Wells and Joel Rubochon's *Simply French*, a recipe for mussels with cream, mushrooms, leeks, and fennel includes these specifications:

½ small fennel bulb, cut in julienne strips
4 mushrooms, brushed clean, cut in julienne strips
2 shallots, minced[26]

The definition for julienne and macédoine of vegetables provided in the handout that Le Cordon Bleu gives its basic cuisine students is as follows:

Julienne:
1) Cut the vegetables into 4 cm (1½″) lengths.
2) Cut the lengths into thin slices.
3) Cut the slices into strips.

Macédoine:
1) Cut the vegetables into convenient sized lengths (block shape).
2) Cut the lengths into 2 cm (1½″) slices.
3) Cut the slices into 2 cm (1½″) strips.
4) Cut the strips into 2 cm (1½″) squares.

Figure 2. Making a julienne of carrots. Even today, the chef's ability to demonstrate a perfect julienne, uniform and consistent, is still important. Copyright Paul O. Boisvert. New England Culinary Institute.

The importance of mastering these skills for the proper execution of the cuisine can be seen in Escoffier's recipe for borscht: "Cut in julienne-fashion the heads of two leeks, one carrot, half of an onion, four ounces of the white of cabbage leaves, half a root of parsley, the white part of a stalk of celery, and four ounces of beets; set the whole to stew gently in butter."[27] Though it would be possible to put all these ingredients into a pot to cook without an understanding of what it means to julienne, both the cooking and the presentation of the soup would be jeopardized. The uniformity in size created by julienning all the vegetables allows for a consistent cooking process and uniform appearance.

Chefs today who were taught by or apprenticed under a French (or French-trained) chef can almost always tell an amusing story about the art of the julienne from the early days of their career. The most frequent anecdote (which I can tell about myself) starts with a large bag of carrots and the dictum, "julienne those carrots." Several hours later, the supervising chef rifles his fingers through the laboriously cut carrots, states, "these are much too big" or "these are much too inconsistent," and promptly dumps them in the trash.

The principles and combinations in French haute cuisine to which chefs adhered became just as important to the diner; the names of the classic dishes, such as saumon à la printanière and consommé à l'impériale, are consistently used in hotel and restaurant menus outside of France throughout the nineteenth and twentieth centuries. For example, at the O. M. J. Association annual meeting at Young's Hotel in Boston in 1883, the menu included consommé à la royale, filet of beef aux champignons, cutlets of lobster à la cardinal, and charlotte russe.[28] Even farther afield, the menu in honor of Sir Saul and Lady Samuel, at the National Park, Sydney, Australia, on May 18, 1888, included dinde rôti aux truffes, mayonnaise de poulet, and crème de meringue.[29]

We do not know whether banquet participants, on reading the menu, comprehended what they would be eating or whether they simply waited for the plate to appear before them to find out that dinde rôti aux truffes is roast turkey with a truffle stuffing. It is clear, however, that during the nineteenth century French culinary vocabulary was considered an acceptable way to describe the evening's menu, whether in France, Australia, Britain, or America. Maybe all the diners needed to know was that the menu was French. That being true, everyone knew exactly where they were—at a fancy meal.

COOKING METHODS

Vital to the French culinary system are the cooking methods, or *les cuissons*. There is a tradition in French cookbooks that the first pages begin with basic definitions for fundamental culinary practices, thus providing a road map for engaging the system. The inclusion of a section on cooking methods is where authors aiming toward female bourgeois and male professional cooks meet: these foundational skills appear to transcend the gender divide. Madame Saint-Ange, author of *La Cuisine de Madame Saint-Ange*, which was called "one of the bibles of French home cooking," has an extended section on cooking methods in her book. Jules Gouffé begins with a similar section in *Le Livre de Cuisine*, and more than one hundred years later Michel Guérard in *Cuisine Minceur* (1976) starts his first chapter with "les cuissons."

Gouffé lists the terms he considers most important to mastering professional cuisine: *blanchir*, *braiser*, *clarifier*, *découper*, among others. Most cookbooks on French cuisine written for an nonnative audience also include definitions of such techniques. In Elizabeth David's *French Provincial Cooking*, braising is defined as when "meat and poultry are . . . cooked very slowly with vegetables, herbs, fat pork or bacon and a small amount of liquid."[30] In *Mastering the Art of French Cooking*, Julia Child includes a section entitled "Definitions" to inform readers about cooking methods. She defines *sauté* in the following way: "To cook and brown food in a very small quantity of very hot fat, usually in an open skillet. You may sauté food merely to brown it, as you brown the beef for a stew. Or you may sauté until the food is cooked through, as for slices of liver."[31] She goes on to explain in detail the reasons people do not sauté properly (the fat is not hot enough, the food is not dry, the pan is too crowded), of concern because it "is one of the most important of the primary cooking techniques."[32]

As Guérard puts it, "whatever method is used, . . . cooking is the process by which food passes from the raw to the cooked state."[33] In reviews of cooking methods, the primary distinction is made between dry-heat and moist-heat methods. Dry-heat methods attempt to seal the juices found in the food; moist-heat methods add moisture with liquids, usually wine or stock. Here the focus will be on two methods: roasting and braising. Roasting is a classic example of a dry-heat method, which dates to the earliest eras of hearth cookery. Braising is a method born, literally, out of the dying embers of the hearth fire. Traditionally, the dish was put in a tightly covered container and placed in the hearth at the end of the day; a low fire of embers slowly cooked the dish overnight.

Brillat-Savarin's Aphorism XV from *The Physiology of Taste* is often invoked in discussions of roasting methods: "We can learn to be cooks, but we must be born knowing how to roast."[34] Unquestionably, proper roasting methods preoccupy those involved with classic French cuisine, and mastery of this method does signal culinary mastery in general. Interestingly, in his section on roasting, Escoffier explicitly refutes Brillat-Savarin's assertion: "I do not say with Brillat-Savarin that a good roaster is born and not made; I merely state that one may become a good roaster with application, observation, care, and a little aptitude."[35] In Escoffier's mind, roasting is another skill to be mastered by the willing apprentice.

How do you properly roast? According to many authors, the first distinction lies in where you roast: on a spit over or near a fire or in a pan in an oven. Many prefer the spit, particularly over a wood fire, for the superior flavor it imparts.[36] Escoffier dislikes the oven because steam can accumulate inside, which affects the flavor and texture of the meat. Nevertheless, by the late nineteenth century, ovens were the norm, and so they aim their directives to the oven roast. Saint-Ange says: "More than any other cooking method, it allows meats to retain their characteristic bouquet and full worth."[37] The relationship between the meat and the internal liquids is most important. As *Larousse Gastronomique* puts it, "the distinctive feature of this form of cooking by concentration is that the internal juices are preserved."[38] Above all, the meat should be seared before it is roasted, there should be no liquid in the roasting pan, and care should be taken not to overcook the meat.

Jacques Pépin in *La Technique*, a cookbook aimed at the American home cook, focuses on explaining *when* a roast is properly cooked, probably a reaction to the historical tendency in America to cook meat until well done. He says, "A professional chef knows by touching, or rather pushing into the meat with his fingers. How the meat springs back clearly reveals the degree to which the meat is cooked."[39] In a much earlier epoch, Dumas in *Le Grand Dictionnaire de Cuisine* (1870) champions the roast over boiled meats; at the time boiling was considered a more healthy cooking method. He argues that roasting allows meats to retain their juices, a more natural approach.[40]

A moist-heat method, braising involves adding liquid to meats, but also fish, poultry, and vegetables, and cooking for a long period over low heat. Child defines *braiser* as follows: "To brown foods in fat, then cook them in a covered casserole with a small amount of liquid."[41] Her recipe for gigot ou épaule de pré-salé braisé (leg or shoulder of lamb braised) follows the methods for a true braise: first the leg or shoulder is seared over a high heat, then liquid and sliced vegetables are added, and the whole concoction is cooked, covered, for three to four hours. Both Child and Escoffier agree that the best braised meats have been marinated for several hours ahead of time, preferably in wine.

For a proper braise, the amount of liquid must be just right. In the "Elementary Methods" section of his book *Ecole de Cuisinières*, aimed at female domestic servants, Urbain Dubois emphasizes this important issue. He believes that "to properly braise meat, one must avoid cooking it in too much or too little liquid."[42] In the first case one ends up boiling the meat; in the second the meat becomes dry. Ingredient proportions also make a difference. Madame Saint-Ange begins her discussion on braising with this emphatic statement: "One will not get good results with a piece of meat that is too small."[43] She also argues that lots of fat is needed for a good braised dish. This can be achieved by larding the piece of meat or by adding small pieces into the cooking process, as in the classic coq au vin. Another concern is having the right equipment for this method to be executed properly. The classic pot is a braisière, oval or rectangular in shape with a tight-fitting lid. Braisières were developed for hearth cookery; classic versions have a concave lid, a design that enabled embers to be placed on top.

The final building block of French cuisine is pastry. In French cuisine, a distinction is usually made between cuisine (cookery) and pâtisserie (pastry). In fact, many professionals choose either cuisine or pâtisserie as an area of specialization; many consider them different forms of expert knowledge. Certain pastries are used in both cuisine and pâtisserie, however, and thus play an important role in French cookery as a whole. Le Cordon Bleu teaches basic pastry in the first weeks of the basic cuisine course, along with the sauces and knife skills mentioned above. Some American culinary schools offer specializations in pastry for the second year of their programs.

All pastry is based on a combination of flour, liquid, and fat. Usually the fat is slowly incorporated into the flour until the mixture resembles a coarse meal; then liquid is slowly incorporated. Finally, the resulting mixture is kneaded until a paste is made. As always with French cuisine, numerous derivations of this basic technique exist. The simplest (in terms of ingredients), which is used in both savory and sweet preparations, is pâte brisée, or short paste. This pastry consists solely of flour, water, and butter. Pâte sucré has the added ingredients of egg and sugar, whereas pâte feuilletée, or puff pastry, differs in its high butter content. A typical savory preparation using pastry would be saumon en croûte, in which a whole salmon is covered with puff pastry and baked in the oven. Pâte brisée can be used for the classic tarte aux pommes, in which apple slices are arranged in a pastry shell and baked.

Professional Chefs and Cookbooks

Text-based knowledge allows for a codified haute cuisine, accessible to all with the desire to learn and a willingness to follow the rules. Oral knowledge, historically more widespread as a means of transmitting culinary information, leaves room for the cook to use intuition as a resource and repetition as a guide. Cookbooks function as utilitarian manuals, providing the necessary knowledge to accomplish a culinary task, yet at the same time sending clear signals about right and wrong practice. Child's dictums "you may, you must" are a case in point.

Over the centuries, the cookbook as a uniform manual of rules, rather than an individual set of notes, became more common. The earliest extant version of Taillevent's *Le Viandier* is handwritten on parchment paper, and only four manuscripts exist today.[44] As well, the increase in more literate, bourgeois readers led to cookbooks becoming a more significant part of the published genre; chefs were more often their authors. Cookbooks become ever more complex in their aims and intents: education, exhortation, information. With a larger body of cookbook readers, this genre had increasing influence on actual cooking practice. By the late nineteenth century, cookbooks had become tomes with important practical but also social messages.

Two cookbooks written in the late 1800s illustrate the broadening scope of the cookbook: Auguste Escoffier's *Guide Culinaire* and *La Cuisine Pratique*, published by Le Cordon Bleu magazine and cookery school. Revealed as well is a new division in the perceived audience for cookbooks: professional male chefs versus domestic female cooks.

Escoffier imagined the audience for his book to be professionals. He called *Le Guide Culinaire* "a practical guide for future chefs of large restaurants."[45] After more than thirty years cooking in restaurants and hotels in France and England, Escoffier, at least partly out of necessity, had made changes to the haute cuisine of his training and wanted to document them.

> The need for this kind of guide became more apparent every day to address the problems of rapid service now becoming current in these kinds of restaurants. I myself have often been forced to make profound changes in my restaurant service to meet the needs of the ultra rapid pace of modern life. For instance, I have had to eliminate pedestals and invent new, simplified ways of laying out and presenting dishes.[46]

Escoffier is credited with reorganizing the professional kitchen by streamlining the production system, in which each cook is responsible for a component of the finished plate. The change in production style forced him to revise many classic techniques and methods. Escoffier's book is comprised of two parts: "The Fundamental Elements of Cooking" and "Recipes and Methods of Procedure." The various components of haute cuisine are covered: "Basic Principles of Cookery," "The Leading Culinary Operations," "Eggs," "Fish and Seafood," and "Desserts and Sweets." Recipes constantly refer to one another, and Escoffier promotes a *system* of cooking, for no dish can be made in isolation in a professional kitchen; all are components of the larger cuisine, or menu. His culinary system can be seen in a recipe for marquis potatoes: "Take one lb. of croquette paste (219) and add six oz. of very red, thick tomato purée (29). Pour this mixture into a pastry bag fitted with a large grooved tube and squeeze it out upon a baking-tray in shapes resembling large meringue shells."[47] The croquette paste recipe, number 219, is fairly exact: "Cook quickly in salted water 2 lbs. of peeled and quartered potatoes. As soon as they seem soft to the finger, drain them, place them in front of the oven for a few minutes in order to dry, and then turn them into a sieve lying on a cloth, and press them through without rubbing."[48] The croquette recipe functions as the master, and Escoffier provides three variations.

When Escoffier moves into the second part of the book, his approach becomes even more analytical. In his section on fish and seafood, he discusses the seven ways of cooking fish: boiling, frying, cooking in butter, poaching, braising, grilling, and cooking au gratin. Each procedure is outlined in detail. For "The Boiling of Fish in Salted Water," he says: "The object of this process is to concentrate, inside the fish, all the juices contained within it, whereas a large portion escapes when the cut fish is plunged in cold water gradually brought to the boil."[49] The fish section concludes with a list of recipes, grouped according to the variety of fish. There are 104 recipes for sole alone, including Florentine, Montreuil, au gratin, and Duglère. The professional has a manual for action which probably does not fare as well in the domestic realm; in order to make sense of *Le Guide Culinaire* and to use it with some constancy, a commitment to the total system must be made.

La Cuisine Pratique is a collection of recipes used at the cooking classes held at the Cordon Bleu School at the Palais Royale. These classes were taught by male chefs and attended by housewives and female domestic servants. The individual recipes and discussions were written by chefs in these two volumes bound into one, but the book was edited by Marthe Distel, who also ran the school. (A lengthier discussion of the school and its importance to French cuisine at the turn of the century will appear in Chapter 6.)

The first recipe in *La Cuisine Pratique* is for boeuf à la mode, and from the onset this book takes on a very different tone than Escoffier's *Guide Culinaire*. The author, chef Charles Durand, writes, "Boeuf à la Mode ... is one of the simplest, but most succulent, dishes passed down to use from the French cuisine of earlier times, when one could find the time to prepare those cooked stews in earthen pots that our grandmothers would bury in the embers of a wood fire and carefully tend all day.[50] With this nostalgic description, he looks back wistfully at a simpler time of cooking, quite a change from Escoffier's didactic discussion of his culinary system.

Figure 3. At the market. From *La Cuisine Pratique*.

And we hear of a grandmother. Written for an audience of women, the chef concedes the role of women in the French culinary tradition. Perhaps the chef can acknowledge that women mastered excellent cooking techniques in earlier days because this dish clearly lies in the realm of domestic, bourgeois cookery. But he does go on to bemoan the disappearance of boeuf à la mode in restaurants (except for Jamet's longstanding Restaurant du Boeuf à la Mode) and the general tendency in his day to prefer a sumptuous table to a flavorful dish.[51] Whatever the true fate of this particular dish, the audience allows the chef to speak in a different voice.

La Cuisine Pratique occasionally contains stories about chefs. One, "Le Secret de Francatelli," discusses the salads he prepared during his tenure at the Reform Club in London. A customer commented on the wonderful aroma that wafted from the salad when it arrived at the table. The secret? Garlic, crushed in the chef's teeth while he tossed the salad. The smell of his breath helped create that indefinable aroma. The piece ends by saying that the customer thanked Francatelli profusely, but remarked that perhaps he would not admire the salads as much in the future.[52]

The aims of the book are revealed as well in the numerous black-and-white line drawings found throughout. Some are typical pictures of haute cuisine dishes, for example, a crayfish salad à la Maintenon piled high on a platter, coated with aspic, decorated with a crown of whole crayfish, and garnished with several sprigs of parsley. Other drawings depict women in their daily culinary activities. One shows a well-dressed bourgeois woman looking at the poultry and game at the open-air mar-

Figure 4. The chef instructs the ladies on the right technique. From *La Cuisine Pratique*.

ket. She is gingerly holding a bird by the tail, while a young woman who is her domestic servant stands several steps behind. Most revealing, though, is another drawing that shows a perfectly dressed, imperious-looking chef giving a cooking demonstration to a group of bourgeois women, paper and pencil in hand. No doubt exists who is the master of this domain.

Initially, haute cuisine emerges from certain locales in France, promoted and produced by a fairly small group of chefs who made their living creating lavish food for their noble patrons. Their promotional efforts after 1750 focused on developing and disseminating a system of cooking that they could control. At the same time, with the publication of their own cookbooks, individual mastery of their system by the apprentice, another chef, or even an eager bourgeois housewife was now possible.

The written word helped chefs move from being anonymous domestics in the homes of the nobility to being experts for the public because now their knowledge could spread anywhere. This culinary knowledge ultimately defined professional cooking practices in the Western world. In this context, French haute cuisine became transportable and thus capable of tremendous impact, via cookbooks and journals and via French chefs. Bourgeois cuisine, always associated with the home, did not travel as early or as far because it was not necessarily associated with expertise.

Though chefs were making different dishes in new ways prior to the nineteenth century, there were still only two avenues for them to ply their trade: as a member of a guild or as the employee of an aristocratic or haute bourgeois household. By 1800, however, the privilege of individual patronage was neither possible nor necessary. The former institutional parameters of the guild and the courts had disintegrated, and therefore cooks and chefs had to reconsider both their professional identity and professional practice. Only in the nineteenth century did the social arenas for food consumption expand and subsequently create new spaces where chefs and cooks could work.

2 THE EMERGENCE

OF THE RESTAURANT

Though the structure and content of French cuisine began to change during the eighteenth century, places of employ for cooks and chefs remained relatively static. La Varenne, author of *Le Cuisinier Français*, was in the household of a nobleman, the marquis d'Uxelles. The dedication of the cookbook reveals the world of chef and patron at that time. La Varenne dedicates the book to the marquis and talks of his own "humble origins," his "indebtedness," and "the honor to practice in your service." He also states, "I dare to say that I have practiced this profession with the great approbation of princes, marshals of France, and infinity of persons of consequence."[1] It was only in the closed world of the aristocracy that a chef de cuisine could practice his craft up until the 1800s, but it was also in this protected environment, under the sponsorship of a figure such as the marquis, who supported La Varenne's new aesthetics of food, that haute cuisine as we know it today was developed and refined.

Increasing urbanism, particularly the growth of the city of Paris, meant that by the 1700s more and more prepared foods were available for sale. They were chiefly prepared by male artisans, who were members of guilds, much like the furniture makers, coopers, and other craftsmen of the time. The guilds regulated their production and oversaw their apprenticeship. Chefs de cuisine, the elite alimentary craftsmen, only slowly began to move out of the noble households and onto the city streets. At the dawn of the new century came new sites for cooking and eating: restaurants. Urban dwellers could earlier purchase already prepared food, but these locales did not have all the attributes that constitute a true restaurant—the method of service, the type of food served, and the clientele. Also, a new type of consumer came along, primarily the urban citizen (usually of Paris), who followed these new restaurants, commenting along the way. For the new urban bourgeoisie, sitting down to a meal became not just an exercise in sustenance but an activity worthy of engagement and commentary. Grimod de la Reynière's *Almanach des Gourmands* (1803) was a guide to Paris restaurants; in 1858 Charles Monselet published *Le Gourmet: Journal des Intérêts Gastronomiques*, whose main intent was to "tell you places you must eat each week, and also places you must avoid."[2]

When elite chefs de cuisine shifted their culinary practice into the public sphere, this was not a move into an unknown frontier empty of products transformed from the raw to the cooked. Evidence of a tradition of roadside stands and cooked-food shops dates to the fourteenth century. A sixteenth-century Venetian ambassador stated: "Do you want to buy your provisions all prepared? The roasters and the pastry cooks, in less than an hour, will arrange a dinner for you."[3] Since at least the eleventh century a group of tradesmen had been involved in the production and distribution of portable foodstuffs both in England and in France. In his *Canterbury Tales*, written in the late 1300s, Chaucer wrote in the Cook's Prologue and Tale about the "victualling trade." In a dialogue with the Cook, the Miller says:

Now tell on, Roger, for the word's with you.
You've stolen gravy out of many a stew,
Many's the Jack of Dover you have sold
That has been twice warmed up and twice left cold;
Many a pilgrim's cursed you more than sparsely
When suffering the effects of your stale parsley
Which they have eaten with your stubble-fed goose;
Your shop is one where many a fly is loose.[4]

Though this is no glowing review of Roger's culinary capacities, we see the dependence of the pilgrim or traveler on the public purchase of prepared food. Later in the Cook's Tale, Chaucer describes a cook's apprentice who "preferred the tavern to the shop" and "Came down to Cheapside, goodbye to his profession!"[5]

From the tenth century on, the growth of towns and the expanding use of money as a medium of exchange in Europe led to the advent of organized trades. These trades, usually involved in craft production, were organized around guilds: "The two forces which joined to create the gilds in the Middle Ages were the tendency toward voluntary association for mutual benefit among craftsmen engaged in the same line of work, and the tendency of governing authorities to encourage association among the craftsmen for purposes of regulation, control, and taxation."[6] The guilds of the weavers of Mainz and bakers of Pontoise were given official state recognition in 1099 and 1162 respectively,[7] and the butchers and bakers of London in 1180 and 1155.[8]

London's Worshipful Company of Cooks became a recognized organization in 1311,[9] though there are earlier recorded mentions of cooks in London. For example, Fitz-Stephen's "Description of London" of 1170 mentions "cookshops" on the Thames, where "at any time of day or night, any number could be fed to suit all palets and all purses."[10] By the end of the fourteenth century, the cooks' guild incorporated cooks, pastlers (makers of pasties), and pie bakers. An important responsibility of the cooks' guild beginning in the fourteenth century concerned the inspection and supervision of cookshops throughout London. Other tasks of the guilds included "i. Control the system of apprenticeship and ensuring and maintaining standards of trade. ii. Regulation for holidays, hours, and to some extent wages and prices. iii. Pageants iv. Charities to Widows, Orphans, and poorer breatheren."[11] The guilds of the City of London retained these responsibilities over trades until the early to mid-nineteenth century.

A similar history of trade guilds exists in France, though all guilds were abolished during the French Revolution. In Paris the guilds were regulated by both the municipal and the royal governments. In the thirteenth century, businesses related to food could be found in the city; a listing of the "métiers d'alimentation" from the thirteenth to eighteenth centuries includes boulangers (bakers), cuisiniers-traiteurs (cook-caterers), rôtisseurs, charcutiers (pork butchers), and pâtisseurs de pain d'épices.[12] From 1200 to 1500 there were very few ordinances that involved the regulation of cuisiniers-oyers, chiefly because in this period cooks were generally classified under the categories charcutiers and rôtisseurs. During the reign of Henri IV (the late 1500s) the métier of cuisinier was confirmed in statutes. The official guild was for "maître Queux, Cuisiniers, Portechappes, et Traiteurs." Interestingly, three of the four occupations— maître Queux, Cuisinier, and Traiteur—figure largely in the invention of the restaurant.[13] Under these statutes, traiteurs had the authority to prepare food for all weddings and banquets.[14] A separate set of statutes for cooks of the grandes maisons, called the "maîtres queux," was written in 1599. The term was gradually transformed by the nineteenth century into the nomenclature that holds through today: "chef" or "chef de cuisine."[15]

As in the case of English guilds concerned with food production, the

French guilds primarily controlled the labor force via an apprenticeship system and maintained standards of quality. The French case is unusually complex, however. In the cooking trade in France, the royal kitchens were not part of the larger guild structure; thus the cooks' guild, or cuisiniers, was not involved at all with the courtly realm, which had its own separate hierarchical system.[16] The long-term existence of a dual set of work environments for those in the cooking trade, with the courtly sphere primarily inventing "fancy" food and the guild/public sphere producing "everyday" food, had tremendous implications for this labor force. By 1800 a precedent existed for differentiation within the trade between varieties of production. In a detailed account of early Parisian restaurants Rebecca Spang argues that the activities of those involved in food trades in Paris were extremely fluid. Most of those individuals were small shopkeepers who were always searching for new ways to create revenue. The written word of the statute may not have been followed to the letter, at least by the late eighteenth century.[17]

Guilds in France and England were always part of the life of towns, and organization and regulation of these trades did not extend into the rural areas. In fact, town craftsmen kept a careful eye on the entrance of "country traders" into their territory.[18] The town-country tension existed throughout the history of the guilds. In a 1633 bakers' company report, for example, members complained that "these Bakers who bake unsized bread are such as are not experienced in bakeing . . . not apprenticed, And do dwell in the Skirte and Suburbes of the Cittye and doo bake any size [weight] not regarding in the true Assize [regulated weight] that ought to be kept."[19] The notion of supervised training, in the form of apprenticeship, was always an important component of the guilds; in fact, it has been called the "backbone of the craft guild."[20] Though it is not clear exactly when the apprenticeship system first began, by 1563 Queen Elizabeth had decreed the Statute of Apprentices, "which laid down that nobody should practice a trade without first undergoing a seven years' apprenticeship to it."[21]

The guilds can be considered the primary "corporate" organization of the victualing trades in both France and England until the nineteenth century, and from the earliest days of such organization training, quality, and control of the productive process were important.

Urban areas became increasingly populous—for example, it has been estimated that by the end of the eighteenth century the population of Paris was at least 700,000.[22] Among these were possibly as many as 10,000 workers in the food industries, with varying levels of involvement in the food system.[23] Thus from the medieval period until the Revolution, more people were certainly involved in the "victualing trade" than those in noble employ. These workers have been characterized as consisting of three groups: ouvriers, manoevriers, and domestics. The difference between ouvriers and manoevriers was the level of skill involved in their work; ouvriers were usually apprenticed and part of the guild structure, manoevriers like bargemen required no specialized training. Domestic workers were a separate category entirely, and included cooks, grooms, housekeepers, and more.[24]

The guilds retained their powers of surveillance and regulation through the 1600s and 1700s in France and England. These powers included control over the apprenticeship system. The 1686 Bye Laws of the Worshipful Company of Cooks set forth numerous edicts that concerned apprentices: "No member could bind an apprentice to himself until he was first presented to the Masters or Governors of the Company at Common Hall" and "No member could have more than two apprentices at one time."[25] They also had the power to fine any members who " 'have for their own private gain and to the ruin of the Company' . . . taught persons who were not bound by apprenticeship to 'raise and make all kinds of Bakemeats and Pyes.' "[26] The maîtres queux of the French noble household had to contend with such occupational parameters when they left the privileges of the domestic realm.

Public Dining in France During the Nineteenth Century

The invention of the restaurant, and later clubs and hotels, had inestimable impact on the production and consumption of food because this new institution combined two hitherto separate phenomena in European society: *commercial* food production and *public* food consumption. "Restaurant" in the original eighteenth-century usage denoted rich meat broths (bouillions, consommés, and soups) that were good for health, and beginning in the late 1760s the word *restaurant* began to signify a type of public institution. Restaurants were known as locales where these broths could both be bought and consumed on the premises. These offerings were, in a sense, an early version of health food, created to serve the customer's "delicate constitution."

As a site for purchasing food, the restaurant arrived fairly late (and initially only to Paris), for as mentioned earlier France long possessed a wide array of shops and artisans that provided food in some form. René de L'Espinasse, in *L'Histoire Générale de Paris* (1887) lists over twenty-five "métiers d'alimentation," including boulangers, cuisinier-traiteurs, rôtisseurs, charcutiers, and poulaillers (chicken sellers). French urban areas, especially Paris, were extremely rich in their food offerings by the late eighteenth century. A bourgeois housewife or a domestic servant could go out into the streets of the neighborhood or to the market (in Paris most likely Les Halles) and easily find excellent food to take home that was already prepared in some way—sausage from the charcuterie, breads and pies from the boulangerie.

The beginnings of the modern restaurant can be found in the shops of traiteurs. The word is usually translated as caterer, though traiteurs historically prepared food and often sold it at their shops, as well as cooking for large special events. With the shop as the center of operations, the average traiteur would have prepared food on hand but would also fill special orders, for example pâtés and savory pies.[27] These came to have heightened significance as Paris became a mecca for artisans and tradesmen from the rural hinterlands who primarily resided in boarding houses or rented furnished rooms from individuals. These young men generally had no access to kitchen facilities and thus frequently bought dinner at the neighborhood traiteur.[28]

Traiteurs created the first restaurants. Initially, they probably wanted to extend their entrepreneurial attempts to feed the new citizens of Paris. Rebecca Spang refutes the oft-told story that "Boulanger" was the traiteur who first invented the restaurant in 1765. Rather, she points to a number of successful traiteurs—Mathurin Roze de Chantoiseau, Nicholas Berger, and Jean-Baptiste LaBarrière—who beginning in the 1760s capitalized on the changing culinary needs of Parisians.[29] With their focus on individual preferences and menu choice, these men heralded a new era of food consumption in Paris and beyond. The Palais-Royale was the home of many of these early restaurants, as well as cafés.

Early restaurateurs created an innovative new form of *menu*, or bill of fare, that transformed dining practices. At the time, if you were a traveler and dining at an inn, you would be seated with others at a large table—a style known as *table d'hôte*. The traditional menu had simply informed the customer of the dishes to be served and the cost of the meal. The new style offered a series of choices.[30] Often, a traiteur would offer a table d'hôte meal at lunch.

For Brillat-Savarin, nineteenth-century gastronome and author of *The Physiology of Taste*,

> A restaurateur is anyone whose business consists in offering to the public a repast which is always ready, and whose dishes are served in set portions at set prices, on the order of those people who wish to eat them.

The establishment is called a *restaurant*, and he who directs it is the *restaurateur*. The list of dishes with their prices is called, quite simply, the *carte* or bill of fare, and the *carte à payer* or check indicates the amount of food which has been ordered and its cost to the consumer.[31]

Brillat-Savarin extols the many advantages of the restaurant and the à la carte menu. The diner could now eat at any time, whereas the table d'hôte system required everyone to eat together at one sitting, as in someone's home. The à la carte menu allowed individual choice: diners could, "according to their tastes, choose a meal solid, light, or dainty."[32] Brillat-Savarin also comments on the welcome benefits for the traveler or anyone else who does not have ready access to a kitchen. Finally, he is enamored by the democracy of the restaurant: "If he has fifteen or twenty francs to spend, and if he can sit down at the table of a first class restaurateur, he is as well off as if he dined with a prince, or more so, for the feast at his command is quite as splendid, and since he can order any dish he wishes, he is not bothered by personal considerations or scruples." Perhaps this is the most important innovation of the restaurant and the à la carte menu: an individual, regardless of social class, has the chance to eat like a king. Cost does concern Brillat-Savarin, and he appreciates the development of reasonable, prix fixe menus that use modest ingredients and can cost just two francs.

The rise of the urban French restaurant, with an à la carte menu brought to the table and waiters to serve the individual wishes of the customer, became definitive by 1804 when Antoine Beauvilliers opened La Grande Taverne de Londres.[33] In this form the restaurant was a French invention and was only transported to other European metropoles later in the century.

Some argue that the restaurant "saved" haute cuisine after the upheavals of the Revolution and the demise of aristocratic rule in France; the shift of the chefs de cuisine into public restaurants guaranteed the survival of this previously exclusive cuisine.[34] I would argue that the restaurant is one of a variety of locales where haute cuisine could flourish, and the existence of a whole array of new spaces for elites to congregate and dine makes a more compelling explanation for its persistence: French haute cuisine was being served in *all* the fancy places, public and private.

This continued elite definition of the cuisine, albeit a definition now much broader in scope, allowed it to thrive. Also, in the new social sites of the nineteenth century, French haute cuisine became simultaneously national and supranational: in these locales haute cuisine became both natural *to* France and representative and symbolic *of* France. A 1906 review of a New York restaurant on Broadway in *The Epicure* discusses the reason for its success: "Each year, at the firm's expense, the chef is sent abroad [to France] in the interest of cuisine in general and to imbibe any new ideas that the French kitchen may present."[35]

By the latter half of the nineteenth century, cooks and chefs had become advocates in this new world of food: their identity and practice were now firmly in the public sphere and among the public. They were professionals now, not domestics. Four groups of people were the primary advocates for French cuisine during the nineteenth century—"the professional male cooks, the restaurant-keepers, the gastronomes and the female cooks employed in the domestic service of the bourgeoisie."[36] Each group had a different interest in "French cooking." The professional male cooks set the standard for the food—methods, technique, ingredients, and presentation—preserving the hauteness of the cuisine, even if the site of creation had shifted.

In fact, over several centuries in Europe, the locations for producing elite cuisine and monitoring the means of production were transformed. Despite such changes, culinary historians have documented the ongoing desire by elites throughout Europe for French haute cuisine. Wheaton discusses the long precedent of French chefs emigrating abroad even before the nineteenth century.[37] She considers the emigration of chefs during the 1600s and 1700s a result of both internal political upheavals and the lure of greater economic rewards. French artisans of all types were in demand among the European courts during this period, and working abroad often meant higher salaries and status. For example, there is evidence that Frenchmen were running kitchens for the nobility in Germany and England.[38] A well-known chef in England during the mid-1700s was Clouet, who worked for the duke of Newcastle, a major figure in the Whig governments of the period.[39] French chefs also went to work for the Russian aristocracy, particularly during the reign of Catherine the Great (1762–96).[40]

By the early 1800s, food entrepreneurs had launched a variety of places to consume food in public. The grand restaurant, which continued to use the à la carte menu but replaced the simple bouillions with the complex dishes of haute cuisine, was one of many choices. Well known grands restaurants of this period were La Grande Taverne de Londres, La Maison Dorée, Véry, and Les Frères Provençaux. Other sites for meals were the café-restaurants, more informal affairs that served buffet lunches, and gargottes or guingettes (translated as "greasy spoon" and "small restaurant with music and dancing").[41] Each place catered to a specific clientele. The early versions of the restaurants, with their healthy soups, have been called the "thinking man's" locale, whereas the gargottes catered to the many laborers working in Paris.[42] In the age of democracy, locales for public eating served as a means for people to create social distinction.

Initially the restaurant was an addition to the array of options available in urban areas. As the public sphere consolidated during the nineteenth century, a haute cuisine could be purchased at shops as well as in grand restaurants. Though many traiteurs plied their trade in small neighborhood shops, some developed a reputation among France's elite. Among these fancier locales was La Maison Chevet, located in the Palais Royal, a mecca for fine dining during the nineteenth century. Founding his establishment soon after the Revolution, Hilaire-Germain Chevet started a long culinary dynasty that lasted throughout the nineteenth century, carried on by his sons and grandsons. Joseph Favre, who worked at La Maison Chevet during the middle years of the century, states in his *Dictionnaire Universel de Cuisine Pratique*: "Chevet was not simply the supplier [of food] to French high society, but also to the high priests of European finance. An array of cooks, respected, respectful, and well disciplined, would execute magnificent work."[43] Favre indicates that Chevet sent cooks all over Europe to create banquets for important business and state functions. An engraving of Chevet's shop from around 1845 shows a chef, dressed in the traditional chef's whites, standing in the entryway. Above him hang whole game and poultry, sausages, and pork hindquarters. To his right are display shelves, and in front of the shop stands an interested gentleman, complete with hat and cane.[44] Auguste Escoffier also worked at Chevet's shop as a general manager for eight months in 1878. During his tenure, La Maison Chevet would send entire meals to England, "a delicate task, as one had to take into account the toll that a possible rough crossing of the Channel would take."[45]

Antoine Beauvilliers was one of the earliest culinary figures to make the transition from being an employee in a royal household to running a restaurant in the public sphere. He founded La Grande Taverne de Londres in the Palais Royal. The reasons he left royal employ are not clear, but his involvement in restaurants began before the Revolution. Notably, Beauvilliers's cookbook *L'Art du Cuisinier* (1814) mentions both areas of employ in the description of the author on the title page: "Antoine Beauvilliers, formerly employed by the Count of Provence, attached to extraordinary royal houses, and presently a restaurateur at the Grand Taverne de Londres."[46] Brillat-Savarin considers him the most important of the early restaurateurs, as "he was the first to have an elegant dining room, handsome well-trained waiters, a fine cellar, and a superior kitchen."[47] Beauvilliers, he comments, was also generous, especially with wine from his cellar, but only until the diner got his bill.

By the time Auguste Escoffier was born in 1846, the transition from the domestic to the public sphere was almost complete. He never worked as a private chef for a member of the nobility, though many of his most loyal customers throughout his career were members of European royal families, including Kaiser Wilhelm and King Edward VII. His years of apprenticeship were in his uncle's restaurant in Nice, Le Restaurant Français, and by 1865 he was in Paris at Le Petit Moulin Rouge, where he worked on and off until 1878. The last thirty years of his career were devoted to bringing haute cuisine to grand hotels.[48]

From early on, women were welcome in Parisian restaurants. The first restaurants provided *cabinets particuliers*, or private rooms where men and women could dine together. An engraving of an early restaurant scene shows a man and a woman walking into the entryway, arm in arm.[49] By the end of the nineteenth century, drawings and photographs show women sitting at tables in large public dining rooms. Women were never found cooking in the restaurant kitchen, however. All evidence indicates that no fine dining restaurant or grand hotel in France had a female cook or chef during the nineteenth century. There are many reasons, but as will be discussed later, the male cooks and chefs who dominated the world of professional cuisine played a large role in the absence of women in the professional kitchen.

Professional cuisine is the grand or haute cuisine of the nobility brought to the streets, the public sphere. Restaurants, hotels, and private clubs are where professionals cook. Vital to the shift from the domestic to the public sphere was the end of patronage as the primary relationship between producer and consumer.[50] The new sites, democratically chosen, altered forever the relation of the elite consumer to the food. The meal had become a commodity, and a complex one.[51] The consumer bought the food, the surroundings, and the service, perhaps reminiscent of buying a ticket to the opera or a ballet.

Throughout the nineteenth century and well into the twentieth, the wealthy and noble class maintained a coterie of domestic servants, including cooks and chefs. However, as the nineteenth-century British gastronome Blanchard Jerrold points out, "The number of rich personages who keep a *grande cuisine* has decreased in both France and England; but a new sphere of activity has been opened to great artists."[52] From 1800 to 1900 the number of chefs in the private sphere dwindled and the number in the public sphere increased. By 1900 the typical chef cooked for a primarily anonymous public. Regular patrons were important to the success of these new establishments; Auguste Escoffier invented dishes for his many dedicated customers—pêche Melba, suprêmes de poulet Georges Sand, salade Victoria.

Artisans involved in food production are essential to the longevity of haute cuisine. In an era preoccupied with equality, a group of workers become champions of the exclusive. To understand the strikingly long history of French haute cuisine is to recognize the fundamental fact that practitioners make this cuisine, literally and figuratively: chefs, traiteurs, cooks. The historical evidence indicates that to examine the power of French cuisine internationally, the unit of inquiry must be the French chefs and not the French nation.[53]

Ironically, these chefs' desire for exclusivity in a world much less dominated by the aristocratic model meant that more people were able to experience the cuisine. Haute cuisine became the privilege of all those who can afford it. The first home for French haute cuisine was the court, but with the passage of time and changes in social and economic institutions, haute cuisine became part of a much broader and deeper configuration of elite culture. In the words of Jerrold, "If the princely kitchens have decayed, the number of people who know how to eat has vastly increased. Clubs [and restaurants] have spread among men a knowledge of refined cookery. The Revolution has democratized the kitchen."[54]

3   THE BRITISH

There is a certain drama to the story of the continuity of French haute cuisine despite the disruption of the traditional sites of production after the Revolution. A major dramatic element is the broad geographical range where French cuisine could be found in the nineteenth century, and found to flourish. Two facts are essential to any understanding of the continued production of French haute cuisine during this period: just as in earlier centuries, the very existence of the cuisine was the result of consumer demand; and the French were not the only interested consumers.

Professional haute cuisine began to be produced outside France within thirty years of the initial innovation that began in Paris; by the 1830s London housed some restaurants and clubs. Therefore, since the beginning, this cuisine has been territorially marked but practically borderless. Its spread was far—New York, London, Rome. The first and always the primary audience for French food was Britain, however, and thus that nation will be used as an example of the pull of France's cuisine beyond France. Understanding the non-French (in this case read "British") consumer's demand for professional (read "French haute") cuisine is important because the French customer cannot be the sole focus when talking about the development and demand for this food.

French haute cuisine in Britain easily migrated outside the most sophisticated noble homes. In the early part of the nineteenth century, it was apparently "only found in some aristocratic households and a small number of London clubs and private hotels," but by mid-century it "had become de rigueur among the fashionable."[1] Why, though, during the height of their own empire, would the British permit a form of French culinary imperialism? Perhaps the British bourgeoisie were "disciplined" into the concession of high cuisine to France because of the limited food and drink options available to them in public. To dine well, the British had to dine French.

During the nineteenth century, new alimentary institutions—pubs, clubs, restaurants, and hotels—arose in Britain to meet the needs of the bourgeoisie, thus increasing options for public consumption. Much as in France, before the 1800s there were few places for the elites to meet outside of their homes, let alone sit down to a proper meal. The local history of the British helps explain the seemingly contradictory reality of a French imperialism in Britain during the latter country's own period of high imperialism.

Public houses, or pubs, were omnipresent in British town and city life during this period. They had evolved partially from the tavern, which was a more "full-service" institution providing lodging, meals, and drinks. The other influence on the nineteenth-century pub was the dram shop, basically a takeout liquor store that provided liquor but no place to sit and nothing to eat. The innovation that helped create the new pub model was the counter: "Introducing a counter immediately introduced the image of a shop where goods were sold over the counter to customers—instead of guests—by shopkeepers who advertised their goods."[2] The pub thus was new in the sense that it was a *commercial* social meeting place whose primary function was to sell a commodity—drinks.

Historically, food was never a very important part of revenues for pubs, nor did people go to pubs with the expectation of purchasing cooked meals. Sandwiches and biscuits were available, and working men often brought their uncooked lunches to the pub to be baked or boiled, but no one worked in pubs solely to prepare food.[3]

By the 1830s, the middle classes were no longer much in evidence at the pubs, which primarily served the working classes. Middle-class ambivalence toward the pub arose in part because members of this class now had other places they could go—clubs, restaurants, and hotels. Social sensibilities played a role as well, as discussed in the *Licensed Victualler's Gazette* in 1888: "In these days when taverns are voted vulgar, it would be almost the ruin of a barrister's reputation to be seen entering a public house unless it were called a restaurant."[4]

Thus, though the pub was an extremely popular public social space during the entire nineteenth century, peaking in the period 1870–1910 (for example, in 1892 there were 7,100 pubs in London alone), the bourgeoisie and elites were not the primary patrons. Other spaces had become their domain. The earliest alternative to the tavern was the gentleman's club. It has been suggested that coffeehouses, which had become a part of London life by the early 1700s, were the precursor to the widespread gentleman's clubs of the 1800s: "From these coffee house 'assemblies,' then the clubs, grew until the time came when every pursuit had its own particular club. They were the refuge of men who cared for fashionable society for enjoyment, and, as a rule, were not inclined to harmful dissipation."[5]

The clubs, with their special interests and their individual invitation cards, began by meeting in the available public spaces—coffeehouses and taverns—and began to take private quarters only in the nineteenth century. These clubs were highly varied in their orientation. Many were organized primarily for political purposes, but some were more whimsical in design. An early twentieth-century gourmet culinary journal, reviewing the history of the gentleman's club, reports: "An important club was the Gentlemen's Bird Fancier Club, and when this organization prepared a feast for its friends, it sent out most imposing cards of invitation. On the card were shown two figures in the long skirted coats of the time, big wigs, and tricorn hats, and these figures were holding a net. One of the figures on the card held a cage in the hand, while the other had a bird fancier's box on his back."[6] During the 1700s the Academy of Music (initially a club) was founded in the Crown and Anchor Tavern on the Strand, and then, appropriately enough, in 1847 the entire tavern was converted into a clubhouse.[7]

As we see in the comment above that characterized the proper man in the club as being "fashionable" yet not too "dissipated" in tastes and habits, the new social sites of this period were not simply rooms bereft of symbolic resonance, nor purely democratic locales. One needed to be a certain type of person to enter a club and, once inside and initiated, a member needed to behave in a certain way. Thus, mere access and participation in one of the new social sites communicated the message of "bourgeois," "upright," and "elite." Perhaps as the social personas of the nonaristocratic residents of London became increasingly differentiated, there was something insufficient about the open milieu of the coffeehouse.

By the 1880s, club life was an established part of the social life of the bourgeoisie and aristocracy when they were in London; in fact, London was considered at the "head of the list." Club life was an international phenomenon; in 1886 it was estimated that more than one hundred clubs, with a combined membership of more than sixty thousand, existed in New York City.[8] Another important aspect of club life was its exclusivity. There is some evidence that taverns and chophouses were frequented primarily by men and that public dining for women in hotels and restaurants did not occur until the 1880s. This was, however, more a result of general social values of the time than of explicit rules and regulations of exclusion.[9] Unlike taverns, which had no fixed clientele and no permanent rules of inclusion and exclusion, the raison d'être for clubs was to bring together like-minded citizens, and to keep everyone else out. The rules of membership varied from club to club, but one rule that was seemingly universally adhered to was the exclusion of women. The reasons for this are many, but the following poem on "Club Life" provides a glimpse of the male attitude toward clubs at the time.

> Life's only a span,
> Says the clubbable man
> While it lasts I will live in its clover;
> In that honeyed retreat
> I can pick what's as sweet
> As the lips of a maid to her lover.[10]

The world of the club, for the "clubbable man," was a place to remove oneself from the cacophony of the outside world (the teeming masses, the nagging wives, the screaming children), a place to relax and engage in everyday sensual pleasures with a group of men of similar rank and station. Needless to say, it was also a place to make important business contacts.

These private clubs, where social events and business meetings could be conducted over leisurely meals, had dining rooms chiefly staffed by Frenchmen. For example, Louis Eustache Ude, who came to England to be chef for the earl of Sefton after having been in the employ of Louis XVI, ended his career at Crockford's Club in St. James, one of the early and important London clubs.[11]

Another club famous for both its politics and its French chefs was the Reform Club. Founded in 1836 by people interested in creating a social environment conducive to those who held Reform, or Radical, rather than Whiggish political views, the club had fourteen hundred members by 1845.[12] Though the original members were primarily liberal politicians, over time men of the professional and literary elites also became members. Henry James and E. M. Forster belonged to the Reform Club during the late 1800s; in fact, James lived there for a time.[13]

Dining Out in England Becomes Dining à la Française

The Reform Club has another claim to fame (at least during the nineteenth century): the quality of cuisine appearing from the large basement kitchens. The club's stellar culinary reputation reveals the profound interconnection between fine dining and French haute cuisine that consolidated in Britain during the 1800s. The club's excellent culinary reputation initially was result of the presence of Alexis Soyer, a French chef who left France during the Revolution of 1830.

The reasons for Soyer's departure are not clear, though James Beard believes he "followed in the footsteps of other famous French chefs who had found the British of the nineteenth century keenly interested in fine food."[14] In *Memoirs of Soyer*, Volant and Warren report a more dramatic set of events. These former secretaries to Soyer report that during the Revolution of 1830 he was working in the French Foreign Office in Paris, and the Revolution "entered the kitchen" in the guise of armed men who "extended their ravages upon all the refined resources of French skill."[15] Whatever Soyer's motivations for coming to Britain, he soon became a culinary figure in London and was known for the elaborate feasts he oversaw at the Reform Club.[16] He was also interested in designing more efficient kitchens; he completely reorganized the club kitchens during his sojourn there. He was interested in simplifying domestic cookery as well. He published numerous cookbooks, including *The Gastronomic Regenerator* (1847), *Soyer's Modern Housewife* (1860), and *A Shilling Cookery for the People* (1855); was involved in humanitarian efforts to feed the poor in Dublin and London; and helped provide nourishing, healthy meals to sick soldiers during the Crimean War. There were other French chefs working in London during the mid-1800s, but Soyer's books and humanitarian deeds made him well known to the English public, and thus he became the "representative" French chef of the time in England.

The influence of this French chef (and his successors, including Charles Francatelli, an Englishman who went to France to apprentice to the great Antonin Carême) can be seen in the banquet cuisine of the Reform Club through the twentieth century. Dinner menu cards were printed completely in French through World War II. Menus from 1900 through 1920 are remarkably similar in form and content. At the dinner for G. H. Ryan, Esquire on November 20, 1905, the seventeen members and guests dined on caviar, tortue claire, chaudfroid de caille à la royale, selle de mouton, sauce groseille, faisans rôtis, and parfait au moka, among other things.[17] At the dinner in honor of Lieutenant Colonel Hope Johnstone on October 3, 1924, the menu is startlingly similar:

consommé au vesiga, côtelette d'agneau Rachel, faisans rôtis.[18] From these menus we can see that throughout the history of the Reform Club, home to the liberal defenders of the English nation and also its cultural elite, the standard, set-piece fancy meal was French in language, French in organization, prepared by Frenchmen, and basically French in taste.

The gentleman's club was an important social space for bourgeois entertaining from the early 1800s; the restaurant had a later start. An 1890 article entitled "Les Restaurants Anglais" that appeared in a special section of *L'Art Culinaire* (a culinary journal for chefs) has this to say about the history of restaurants in London:

> In London, proper restaurants have only existed for the last thirty years. Before that time, one couldn't find establishments of this type, only fixed price menus in "public houses," bars where you could eat, standing up, the plate of the day garnished with vegetables boiled in water, chop houses where the client was only served chops and beefsteaks, and cookshops or "boutiques de charcutiers" where you could only procure roast meat or soup.[19]

The important distinction being drawn is between various institutions that served food before 1855 that do not count as "restaurants à la Française," and subsequent institutions that do. There is a particular model for a restaurant; simply being a place for public consumption of food is not sufficient. Another set of criteria must be met.

For the authors of this article (chefs and journalists from France), an eating establishment can be considered a "restaurant Anglais" if it resembles Le Café Royal on Regent Street: "un restaurant essentiellement français." Apparently there is no antinomy in such an analysis for these Frenchmen—they found what they were looking for in an establishment of one of "our compatriots, Monsieur Nicol." They were not the only ones to give a stamp of approval to this restaurant. It is reported that Le Café Royal employed about two hundred people, including thirty cooks under the direction of a French chef, Monsieur Garnier.[20] The London diner of the 1880s and 1890s was as appreciative of the French restaurant as the French critic.

By 1890 there were five thousand French chefs involved in all forms of elite cookery in Britain.[21] The Prince of Wales had a French chef, Monsieur Menager, and working under him were three other cooks "également Français." His sons the dukes of Clarence and Connaught had French chefs in their employ. The embassy kitchens were primarily staffed by Frenchmen—Monsieur Augustin at the Russian Embassy, Monsieur Barre at the Austrian Embassy, Monsieur Menessier at the

Danish Embassy. In the world of finance, all four houses of the Roth-schild family were served by the French; the homes of such nobles as Lord Shrewsbury and Lord Salisbury employed French chefs as well.[22]

The king and queen, the highest representatives and upholders of Britain and British culture, had French food at their banquets at Buck-ingham Palace. One banquet menu had ten courses, including tortue claire, chaudfroid de volaille à la Bagration, and macédoine de fruits au champagne.[23] French chefs or British chefs trained in French cuisine generally held the highest position in the royal palace.

Grand hotels—the Ritz and the Savoy for example—were another locale where French chefs consistently worked in London. The develop-ment of luxury hotels that functioned not as mere resting places during a long journey but as destinations in themselves was an international phenomenon beginning primarily during the 1800s. The earliest versions were situated near thermal baths (Carlsbad, Baden-Baden), but soon luxury hotels became a part of the Riviera (Monte Carlo, Nice) and were places where the wealthy could "take a cure."[24] By the 1870s they were found increasingly in major metropolitan centers: New York, Paris, London. In fact, the developer of the Savoy Hotel in London, Richard D'Oyly Carte (also known for his role as the manager and producer for Gilbert and Sullivan), was inspired by his experience of the "higher stan-dard of comfort in the best New York hotels."[25]

D'Oyly Carte had clear ideas about the social space he wanted to create for elite Londoners, ideas that included the introduction of fine dining, for even by 1889 "it was not a habit of what was called 'Society' to dine out for the sake of dining out." He wanted to develop a restaurant that was part of the larger hotel but also had a reputation in its own right—to make dining in his restaurant "akin to a performance."[26] In-cluded in his dramatic ambitions for the Savoy restaurant were distinct ideas about the food. The food should draw people to the restaurant, and the quality of the meals should make them return, again and again. He decided that French cuisine would be served at the Savoy.[27]

D'Oyly Carte's initial attempts to create his glittering new social milieu were not a success because neither his general manager nor his chef (who had previously worked for the Rothschilds) had any experience running an à la carte restaurant.[28] But a year after the Savoy opened, D'Oyly Carte went to Baden-Baden to "take the waters," and made the acquaintance of César Ritz, whom he hired to be the general manager. Ritz brought with him from the Continent several people, including Echenard as maître d'hôtel and, more important, Auguste Escoffier as chef de cuisine.

Escoffier, now heralded as the most important figure in the creation of the public profession of chefs, did some of his most innovative work during his sojourn at the Savoy from 1890 to 1898. He was responsible for the invention of many new dishes. The synergy between Escoffier's culinary ideas and the locales where they were put into practice is lovingly described by Marie Ritz, wife of César Ritz, in her discussion of his cookbook, *Le Guide Culinaire.*

> Escoffier's *Culinary Guide* is something more to me than a superior sort of cookbook. I turn the pages of it, and it is like turning the pages of my own personal history . . . mine, and my husband's. *Mousseline de Volaille Patti . . . Poularde Tosca. . . .* Ah! Those hark back to Savoy days. . . . *Filets de Sole Véronique. . . .* I recall the theatrical supper party at the Carlton for which that was created. . . . *Coeurs d'Artichauts Grand Duc . . . Consommé Vladimir. . . .* Those dishes first came out of the Hôtel Ritz kitchens.[29]

The culinary system Escoffier outlined in the cookbook, which eventually became a manual of proper practice for professionals throughout the twentieth century, was inspired by the elite patrons who frequented his restaurants.

Escoffier was also a key player in the reorganization of the professional kitchen. The change in the way food was produced, essentially a breakdown of labor into a series of specific tasks (hence the different stations with different responsibilities—saucier, rôtisseur, pâtissier), allowed for a more expedient and intensive process. The relationship between the individual cook and the craft of cooking was transformed: no single person created the final product; rather, everyone was part of a team. As Mennell has pointed out, these practices resembled "in microcosm, the same trends as were unfolding in the industrialising economy at large."[30]

Changing economic trends affected consumption practices as well as the organization of production. In the case of the Savoy Hotel, we see the confluence of these changes. As Escoffier observed, "the restaurant of the Savoy Hotel became the rendezvous for the elegant world: here, each night one could find the greatest of the English and foreign nobility, the high priests of finance, and celebrities of the art world."[31] And these elites were participating in their social functions all over the world. At its late nineteenth-century peak, the Ritz-Carlton Hotel Group had hotels in London, Paris, Budapest, Rome, Naples, Buenos Aires, Evian, Lucerne, Rapallo, Boston, New York, Philadelphia, and Atlantic City![32] These sites of sociality reflected, but also reinforced and reproduced, the changing economic and cultural organization of the society at large.[33]

Two phenomena were occurring simultaneously in the new eating and drinking locales of the nineteenth century. On the one hand, these places were being used to facilitate the assertion of class difference among British citizens: the artisan went to the pub for his pint and sandwich, and the barrister went to his club for sherry and consommé de tortue claire. On the other hand, once the appropriate place had been decided on and the doorway crossed, further issues of discernment and conviviality were resolved within the chosen social milieu. As Mary Douglas puts it: "Consumption means nothing if it does not mean that some physical things in the end get consumed. But let us realize that the services they yield are of two kinds, one the enjoyment of physical consumption, the other the enjoyment of sharing names . . . that have been learnt, distinguished, and graded."[34] In other words, there was a social hierarchy along class lines of particular public eating and drinking places. Beyond the structuring of social relations, however, the consumables contributing to this demarcation were themselves subject to a structuring and shaping process.

For the British elites during the nineteenth century, French haute cuisine as a commodity in the public sphere effectively and symbolically encapsulated culture, or the bourgeois concept of elite culture. At the same time, haute cuisine did not come in a discrete and concrete package.[35] Nor was haute cuisine a free-floating phenomenon, unconstrained by space and time; rather, the production and consumption of French haute cuisine occurred in certain milieus and not in others. And, finally, someone had to make this commodity and, given the nature of cooking as a practice, that person was not far from the consumer. Thus the cook fulfilled a symbolic need as well: it was not just French cuisine, but also French chefs the consumers desired.

The cuisine was able to move from France and have resonance in Britain because French haute cuisine was attached to a particular set of meanings, as well as to a particular set of places. In other words, French haute cuisine as it moved into the public sphere possessed a "social life."[36] First, as food, it functioned as nourishment, helping to prolong human lives. But defining haute cuisine as "food" is like describing Versailles as "a big building": myriad levels of meaning are erased in the association of a thing with its lowest common denominator. French haute cuisine amounts to much more than a list of ingredients. Its social life as food-as-commodity rather than just food occurs because the dish, the meal, and the banquet are in fact a package of goods and services. This package includes the transformation of ingredients into food, then elite food, and finally professional cuisine. Consumed within the protected walls of the royal courts and noble homes in earlier times, haute cuisine as a commodity happens within a particular "regime of value,"[37] when the cuisine is desired by certain people and is eventually consumed by these people in the public domain. Finally, haute cuisine transcends political boundaries, even though the commodity itself is understood to have a specific national culture of origin. Would the bourgeoisie have gone to a pub for chaudfroid de volaille? If such a dish were served at the Angel in Islington, a vastly popular pub in North London, would it still have been a pub? Probably not.

Whether they chose to participate or not, the average British bourgeois saw the world of fine dining to be a world created and ruled by the French. Such an idea helped to create a wide-open arena for French haute cuisine in Britain. The abdication of high cuisine to the French appears to have met with some resistance, however, as witnessed by certain manifestations of ambivalence (see Chapter 4). The British attitude toward French cuisine vacillated between two widely held social beliefs of the Victorian era: moral superiority and cultural inferiority.

Thus the bourgeois public sphere in Britain during the latter 1800s included these sites of public interaction and consumption. These sites were places to relax with your peers, display your wealth, express discernment, make business contacts, and enjoy sensuous pleasures. But when it came to food they were also heavily imprinted with the stamp of the French.

4 CULTURAL NATIONALISM

The metropolis of London exceeds Paris in extent and population; it commands a greater supply of all articles of consumption, and contains a greater number and variety of markets, which are better supplied. We greatly surpass the French in mutton, we produce better beef, lamb and pork and are immeasurably superior both in the quantity and quality of our fish, our venison, and our game, yet we cannot compare, as a nation, with the higher, the middle, or the lower classes in France, in the science of preparing our daily food.—A. V. Kirwan, 1864[1]

French haute cuisine with necessary ideas and skills has survived over three centuries because there were people interested in savoring the products of its masters. Consumer demand continued during the nineteenth century despite profound transformations in the organization of European society during that epoch: the diminishment of the autocratic state and its gradual replacement by the democratic nation-state, the advent of industrialization, and the expansion and subsequent entrenchment of a social order based on class distinction.[2]

The British were enthusiastic consumers of French haute cuisine. The tremendous flow of technical information, practitioners, and institutions involved with French cuisine to other locales during this period is also striking, but it is useful to study the British experience as an example of this French influence. As noted earlier, up to five thousand French chefs were living and working in Britain by 1890.[3] The reasons for such influence lie in more than the finesse of a perfect béchamel.

The Baleful Cosmopolite

Why was French haute cuisine able to move so successfully beyond its culture of origin and dominate British fine dining establishments? One of the most dramatic changes in nineteenth-century European society was the tremendous increase in the number of people understood to be members of the bourgeois class; more than one commentator has called this time the Bourgeois Epoch. In the century between 1790 and 1890 a new category of consumers came into existence, participants in an array of new consumption practices.[4] Social historians have begun to examine seriously the rise of consumer culture among the European bourgeoisie during this period. Fine dining experiences were one part of a constellation of new bourgeois activities: other components included shopping at department stores, going to theatrical events, and traveling abroad. It is to these consumers that we must turn to understand the ongoing history of French haute cuisine, and French haute cuisine in Britain.

Henry James's "Occasional Paris," written in 1883, is a helpful tour guide through the terrain of the nineteenth-century bourgeoisie. In this essay, he is intrigued by the bourgeois traveler, ostensibly world-weary but not yet so blasé as to have lost his critical faculties. James begins the essay by noting:

> It is hard to say exactly what is the profit of comparing one race with another, and weighing in opposed groups the manners and customs of neighboring countries; but it is certain that as we move about the world we constantly indulge in this exercise. This is especially the case if we happen to be infected with the baleful spirit of the cosmopolite—that uncomfortable consequence of seeing many lands and feeling at home in none. . . . There comes a time when one set of customs, wherever it may be found, grows to seem to you about as provincial as another; and then I suppose it may be said of you that you have become a cosmopolite. You have formed the habit of comparing, of looking for points of difference and of resemblances, for present and absent advantages, for the virtues that go with certain defects, and the defects that go with certain virtues.[5]

How do we relate James's portrait of the cosmopolite, so knowledgeable of the world's complexities that distinctions must constantly be made, and Kirwan's earlier, more anxious description of food habits in London and Paris? Common traces can found in their usage of the rhetoric of cultural nationalism; somehow the *difference* between the two places helps create explanations.

Best known as a novelist, Henry James was also a journalist. During the 1870s and 1880s he earned a living writing literary reviews and travel articles for such magazines as the *Atlantic Monthly* and the *Nation*. He spent much of this period traveling through Europe and writing essays on places like Venice, Paris, Rouen, and London for his American readers. Throughout his life, James considered himself both an outside observer of other nations and a cultural commentator on his own.[6] The impact of James' inside-outside stance in his writings is clear in his description of the traveling cosmopolite, who knows so much that he must, inevitably, engage in categorization and comparison. James's insight in the passage above—that knowledge, understanding, or appreciation of one place seems always to evolve in relationship to knowledge, understanding, or appreciation of another—is an invaluable insight into the preoccupations of urban British bourgeoisie of that era.

The intrigue of place, particularly someplace else, is not new. Tales of travel in the guise of quests, pilgrimages, journeys, and voyages appear in all eras and epochs: Ulysses' adventure in the Western Sea, Emperor Mu's tour of the world, medieval pilgrimages to the Holy Land, Columbus's search for India.[7] These, however, are stories of unusual events and adventurous travelers. In the Western hemisphere by the nineteenth century, traveling had become more than a unique story: it was a necessary part of the bourgeois lifestyle. Journeys to the Continent, for example, were a rite of passage for elite Britons and Americans. One is reminded here of the trip young Lucy Honeychurch takes to Florence with her maiden aunt Charlotte Bartlett in Forster's *Room with a View*. Italy was a long journey away from England, but exploring the cultural riches of the Continent was an obvious option for the Honeychurch parents, who were trying to educate their young, unmarried daughter appropriately for her station in life.

James's comments on the importance of comparison to the knowledgeable traveler's awareness of nations and cultures has implications for anthropologists concerned with the construction of culture and cultural categories across space and time.[8] Anthropologists, who were for such a long time subscribers to Samuel Johnson's view that "the use of travelling, is to regulate imagination by reality, and instead of thinking how things may be, to see them as they are,"[9] have themselves recently begun to reconsider their empiricist orientation. As James's comments reveal, anthropologists have never been the sole guardians of the quest for comparative knowledge. In fact, as an anthropologist reading the commentaries of the nineteenth-century British and French on numerous topics, but especially those topics related to elite culture, I find that cultural comparison was a widespread national activity. At the same time, the lack of anthropological analysis of the nineteenth-century concept of culture as elite culture seems a strange omission. Of late, however, anthropologists have turned their analytical gaze to European ideas of elite culture, departing from the inclusive definition that has historically been their domain.[10] Interestingly, considering the comparisons made between British and French cuisine during this period requires both relativistic and exclusionary definitions of culture.

The Idea of a Place

The English perception of France as a locus of sophistication did not arise simultaneously with democracy, capitalism, and new print technologies. The power of the French culture of civility predates the French Revolution; the French court was extremely influential for European courtly society.[11] During the reigns of Louis XIV, Louis XV, and Louis XVI the elaborateness of the royal table was well established. At a royal dinner for fifty people in 1747, the menu included ten grand entrées, twelve terrines, forty-eight entrées, ten grand entremets (display pieces), twenty-four medium entremets, twenty roast platters, and twenty-four salads. The types of dishes at these large banquets were as extravagant as their sheer quantity. The grand entrées included wild boar, lamb, and deer; the entrées included pheasant, pigeon, and turkey; the grand entremets included sausages and pheasant pâté.[12] As in the medieval period, the vast array of dishes was more for purposes of display—both aesthetic and social—than for actual consumption. Many dishes would be returned to the kitchen untouched.

Such opulence extended to the settings and decorations of the royal tables. Porcelain, manufactured under royal supervision at Sèvres, was renowned for its elegance and delicacy: the French king often gave dinner services as presents to royal visitors. In 1758 alone, Louis XV gave sets of Sèvres to the king of Denmark and the emperor of Austria.[13] All the courts of Europe between 1600 and 1800 had an ambassador whose primary charge was to find and acquire for the court the artistic marvels of the day. In matters of table they turned to France, as did king John of Portugal when searching for gold and silver table decorations.[14]

As Norbert Elias notes, in taking over French etiquette and Parisian ceremony, the various rulers obtained the desired instruments to express their dignity, make the hierarchy of society visible, and make all others, first and foremost the courtly nobility themselves, aware of their dependence on the king. But Paris was important as the center of civility not only for members of the court. Beginning in the Middle Ages, this model extended beyond the courtly sphere into "the upper stratum of the bourgeoisie and to some extent even broader layers of the middle class."[15] By the nineteenth century, the European bourgeoisie were simultaneously using two definitions of culture to help maintain their social identity: cultural nationalism and elite culture.

The Expositions Universelles and Great Exhibitions, where the art and industry of many nations were placed on display for the public, were ideal events for the dissemination of ideas about the relationship between cultural nationalism and elite culture. Competitiveness between Britain and France in the areas of trade and industry as well as the fine arts was of long standing. The exhibitions were new arenas for such nationalist jousting. Some scholars argue that France's fine arts exhibits were consistently stronger than Britain's because the French state was investing heavily in the arts to fulfill a "vision of itself as the leader of civilization."[16] Britain focused on industrial might and France on artistic skill. Promotion of France as the locus of "high art" at these exhibitions was a success, as seen in the comments of a reviewer in the *Daily Mail*: "The differences are striking, and are no doubt based on national temperament. There is more genius among the French, more dazzling skill of brushwork, more bravura; while the English art is more delicate in its search for beauty, more pleasing."[17]

In a consideration of the importance of French haute cuisine to the British bourgeoisie, there is no doubt of the important connection between ideas about civilization, art, and elite culture, on the one hand, and eating and cooking practices, on the other. The aristocracy may have lost its power to rule and conquer, but images of France (particularly Paris) as the home of civility and elite culture remained. The author of *Clark's Pocket Paris* (1901) puts it well: "Paris is like a belle of the ball-room. She dazzles with her beauty, her elegant toilet, and with her brilliant repartees."[18] The belief that the definition of culture, civilization, and the bourgeoisie are intertwined crystallizes in the postrevolutionary nineteenth century.

The Idea of French Haute Cuisine

It is interesting to consider characterizations of French cuisine by British bourgeois consumers, given the long-held reputation of France as the home of elite culture and civility. Lieutenant Colonel Nathaniel

Newnham-Davis was involved in producing a new genre of gastronomy in Britain. He was hired by the *Pall Mall Gazette*, a daily newspaper with a circulation of approximately 12,250 by 1890,[19] to write a food column that would "supply useful guidance to persons wanting to know where to dine and what they would have to pay."[20] These columns were compiled into a book, *Dinners and Diners*, which was published in 1899. In 1903 Newnham-Davis with Algernon Bastard published *The Gourmet Guide to Europe*. Both books are gastronomical guidebooks, combining general commentary on dining in restaurants with practical information such as addresses, sample menus, and costs. Newnham-Davis did not rank the restaurants in his discussion. (In fact, the ranking system, which carries so much weight today, was not established in the *Guide Michelin* until the 1930s.)[21] The extensive and descriptive commentary in these books reveals much about the British diner and British ideas and values toward eating and dining at that time.

The subtitle to *Dinners and Diners*, *Where and How to Dine in London*, reveals Newnham-Davis's stance as an instructor, or in his own words, someone who is "preaching a sermon." He does not assume that all the readers know about ordering and dining in a restaurant: he begins by telling the "experienced diner" to proceed straight to the restaurant reviews because his initial words are for the "simple Briton." His strongest piece of advice for his simple reader is to rely on the maître d'hôtel.

> Mr. Echenard, late of the Savoy, in chatting over the vagaries of diners, shook his head over the want of knowledge of the wines that should be drunk with the various kinds of food. No man knows better what goes to make a perfect dinner than Mr. Echenard does, and as to the sinfulness of Britons in this particular, I quite agreed with him. In Paris no man dreams of drinking champagne, and nothing but champagne, for dinner; but in London the climate and the taste of the fair sex go before orthodox rules.[22]

The expert in these matters is the French maître d'hôtel, and the problem, according to him (and Newnham-Davis), is the ignorance (breaking rules) and vulgarity (champagne) of the London diner. This criticism does not extend to all members of the British nation; the problem is severe enough already among the cosmopolitans.[23] The hopelessness of the British diner (and the British cook) is a repeated theme in the culinary literature.

For British writers on the subject during this period, the British incompetence in matters culinary seems to be a matter of comparison. In

Newnham-Davis's *Gourmet Guide to Europe*, the first paragraph of the first page states: "Paris is the culinary centre of the world. All the great missionaries of good cookery have gone forth from it, and its cuisine was, is, and ever will be the supreme expression of one of the greatest arts of the world."[24] *Clark's Pocket Paris*, interspersed with suggestions on where to eat and stay in Paris, explores the culinary differences between London and Paris:

> It is not only at the grand restaurants and hotels that one eats well in Paris. Seeing the high prices obtainable, it is not surprising that some of the greatest chefs and maîtres d'hôtel of France are to be found in London, and with price no object probably the highest class dinner would at present be obtained in London: but step out of this golden band in London, which at most includes twenty restaurants, and you at once fall into a vulgarity of cookery and an insipidity of taste which are unworthy of the name of *cuisine*.[25]

Charles Elme Francatelli, apprentice to Carême, in the preface to his widely published cookbook *The Modern Cook: A Practical Guide to the Culinary Art in All its Branches* (1880) comments:

> Need it be wondered at, while we possess in England a greater abundance of all kinds of food, generally of far better quality than is to be found elsewhere, that our cookery, in theory and practices, has become a by-word of ridicule, and that we should be compelled to have recourse to foreigners, ignorant for the most part of our tastes and habits, to prepare our feasts? "They manage these things better in France": cookery is there considered an important art, and its successful endeavors are regarded with a due appreciation. In Paris its great professors have achieved an almost historical celebrity, and their school of cookery has become preeminent.[26]

Harriet deSalis writes about French cuisine with middle-class assurance in *The Art of Cookery* (1898), even if her analysis of the problem seems remarkably similar to that of the cosmopolitan and the chef:

> It is universally acknowledged, as a fact, that in every class of life our food is not so good as that of foreigners. They live much better abroad, and much more economically, and yet, as materials go, we English are much better off. Now, the chief cause is this: "Cooking is an *art* in France, and is better, therefore, understood."[27]

Through her cookbook, deSalis hoped to improve the cooking skills of all British housewives:

"In England people eat to live, in France they live to eat" is an old saying. Cookery is almost unknown as an art amongst our poor classes, and it is so necessary that the English housewife should learn to make the most of what is at her command. Voltaire used to remark about English cookery, "that though we have 24 religions, we have only one sauce."[28]

If the texts quoted represent prevalent attitudes, then the British believed that the French were more proficient in cookery and that the French nation had some sort of claim to culinary superiority, a claim it particularly deserved when considered in contrast to the "ridiculous" cookery of the English. As Blanchard Jerrold observed in *Epicure's Yearbook* (1868), "The French cook is the King of Cooks because he is of a nation of cooks. Some kind of fine taste is perceptible in the kitchens of all classes in France."[29]

Definition of the Bourgeoisie

It can be difficult to define exactly who were the bourgeoisie in the nineteenth century. Elias's definition, "the privileged town-dwellers,"[30] is vague and probably stems from the initial usage of the word in France during medieval times to characterize good citizens involved in trade. Marx's idea of bourgeois society also stemmed from a view of the bourgeois as "a growing class of traders, entrepreneurs and employers."[31] Engels's definition is more starkly drawn: "By bourgeoisie is meant the class of modern Capitalists, owners of the means of social production and employers of wage laborers."[32] The term "bourgeois" best represents the latter part of the nineteenth century because it reflects the increasing domination of bourgeois society more generally under the capitalist mode of production; as Marx states: "our epoch [is] the epoch of the bourgeoisie.[33]

The period between 1870 and 1910 was part of the Bourgeois Epoch, a time when British society was characterized simultaneously as "carrying light and civilization into the dark places of the world" and "the long garden party."[34] In terms of what Marx and other social commentators of the time called "the upper ten thousand," the advent of industrialization created many changes in what constituted membership. Until 1850, to be a member of London "society" and participate in the season, that "round of social engagements, balls, soirees, dinner parties, formalized social calls, and presentations at court,"[35] it was necessary to own land. By the 1880s the necessary credentials to be a member of London society were less earthbound: "the possession of some form of power over people."[36] This "power over people" could be seen in two ways: the capitalists' extraction of human labor for financial resources, and the bourgeois desire for methods of social and cultural distinction. Elias has argued that such changes in political and economic structures were also instrumental in profound social transformations. He discusses how "the wave of civilization transforms those who fight, eat and sleep on horseback into citizens who cultivate themselves by cultivating their table manners."[37] This combination of political-economic transformations and new views on practices and behaviors can be seen in the British cultural ethos of both moral superiority and social opulence that ruled among the bourgeoisie. Entertaining grandly was part of this civilized world. Dinner parties and restaurant rendezvous created the social arena needed to exhibit glamour and status, because it would be difficult to maintain class rank without the public exhibition of one's ability to consume in an appropriate fashion. Dining was often involved in these conspicuous displays, so the food itself was of great consequence.

For the upper ten thousand, whose numbers now included coal and rail magnates, bankers, lawyers, and other people whose rights to membership in London society had no genealogy in the soil or traditions and whose privileges were thus tenuous at best, the role of cultivated consumer became a vital part of class identity. And in the public realm of the metropole, where food was always a commodity and had become more than a consumable, when Frenchness became attached to it, it became a class marker and cultural icon. In Britain, to have a fine meal was to have a French meal: "civilization" and "culture" coalesced around this cuisine.[38]

British Ambivalence

The British of the nineteenth century cannot be characterized as blind Francophiles; in fact, the British generally have had a love-hate relationship with their French neighbors. Their exercises in comparison had a strong moral component as well, as befitted a country and an era that combined imperial rule with missionary zeal. This cultural ambivalence certainly extended to French cuisine. Hannah Glasse, an eighteenth-century apostle of plain, economical English cookery, does not have nice things to say about the French in the introduction of her classic *Art of Cookery Made Plain and Easy* (1745). She asserts, "if gentlemen will have French cooks, they must pay for French tricks," and, "So much is the blind folly of this age, that they would rather be imposed on by a French booby, than give encouragement to a good English cook!"[39] Though the presence of Frenchmen and French haute cuisine was readily accepted by the British in general, if Glasse is any representative, it appears that not all the British were enamored with France, especially when things French were considered the embodiments of decadence. In his guidebook *Where and How to Dine in Paris* (1900), Strong goes even farther in his analysis of the British attitude toward France: "At the bottom of their souls—dans le creux de leurs estomacs—English people do not like French cooking one little bit, and they disapprove on moral and philosophic grounds of everything else which is really French."[40]

The editors of the British trade magazine *The Caterer and Hotel Proprietor's Gazette* reproduce an editorial from a newspaper columnist who endeavors to refute the French claim to fine food. They introduce it with a bemused tone: "The verdict of competent gastronomical authority is against us, and it is idle to contend that it is unjust, for the general consensus of opinion points all the other way. Nevertheless, the article, which we subjoin, is well worth reading." The article argues that the British have infinitely superior ingredients (oysters, fish), which allows for superior cuisine. Soup is also a topic of discussion: "The lighter sort of French soups, especially sorrel soup, and the frivolous potages made with the tasteless produce of early Algerian springs, have been sometimes praised; but how can they seriously be named the same day with our august real turtle, our royal oxtail, our princely Mulligatawny, and our family pea, with a judicious sprinkling of mint and fried sippets deftly cut."[41]

A powerful middle-class ethos of individual and social morality during the Victorian period is an important clue to understanding the Britons' clearly ambivalent feelings toward the French. In fact, one social historian has stated that the second half of the nineteenth century was "an age when there was a moral coloring to all social argument."[42] The moral stance toward food by the Victorian bourgeoisie resonates with other powerful, morally informed attitudes, particularly the civilizing of the working class and the colonial natives. During the 1870s and 1880s, philanthropic work by the upper classes included the development of soup kitchens for the urban poor and cooking classes to help teach working-class women healthful and economical cookery. But the incomplete British control over food for their civilizing crusade is apparent in Newnham-Davis's comment that "all the great missionaries of good cookery have gone forth from Paris." The seemingly contradictory stances of reverence and disdain that the British had for French cuisine may have arisen from their suspicion that when it came to good food, the French of all people were the ones doing the colonizing and civilizing on British soil.

In the gastronomic literature of Britain, the habit of national comparison seems to be inevitable, even necessary, to make a point about Britain or France. Also, the contrast needs to have a quality of ranking in order to arrive at a set of national defects and virtues. In the case of cuisine, France, despite detractors who decry its reputation as decadent or empty or undeserved, is seen as superior in form and content. The British adopted a morally superior stance to the cultural superiority of the French in order to retain some semblance of comparative power. With such a stance, art, civilization, and culture, and all the "high" cultural productions such as cuisine could be conceded to the French. In the cultural nationalistic discourse of the time, that the French were artistically superior was accepted, but that was all.

Without consumer demand, no real rationale for the availability of either fine or French food in Britain exists. But, as Benedict Anderson reminds us, "the bourgeoisie [are] a world-class in so far as it is defined in terms of relations of production."[43] The consumption of French haute cuisine remains specific to the elite and bourgeoisie of Britain. The attitudes of cultural nationalism revealed in discussions of art, cuisine, and civilization were not held by every Briton and Frenchman of the period: this was the cultural nationalism of the haut monde. The desire of the British bourgeoisie in the nineteenth century to establish and confirm class identity, and their need to view themselves as "cosmopolites," play a pivotal role in French haute cuisine's becoming part of British eating practices.[44]

It is necessary to look farther than the attitudes and values of consumers toward France and French culture more generally in order to understand the ready acceptance of French haute cuisine in Britain, at least at the level of elite culture. Bourgeois consumers held French cuisine in high esteem partly because of the historic importance of things French in the courtly sphere. But that does not explain the continued power of haute cuisine throughout the nineteenth century, as imperialism and nationalism were becoming increasingly important factors in shaping the British nation and British social identity. During 1870–1910 the British were at the height of their political and economic power. Their lethal combination of real might and a general cultural sense of superiority can be seen in the many ways rule, control, and power are indicated in the phrase "the sun never sets on the British Empire."

There is an ironic element to the passive, almost slavish attitudes of the British toward French cuisine during a period when Britain was at the peak of its imperial power. Given such power, could a generalized sense of inadequacy in the realm of cooking be sufficient cause for the rule of France in the public British kitchen? Cooking seems to have been one area of British culture where its citizens' sense of power dissipated. Though the British could disrupt the lives of entire populations of people and transform the terrains of colonies to obtain the raw ingredients— sugar, coffee, spices—they appear to have believed their hands were tied when it came to the transformation of nature into culture.

If the literature on food is used as a window on the attitudes of a larger social arena, the nineteenth-century bourgeois British agree on a clear and obvious difference between Britain and France. But within the larger, generally conflict-ridden, and distrustful relationship between the British and the French, there are moments of engagement and, in the case of cuisine, acceptance and incorporation.

The assumptions about place in the gastronomy books and cookbooks of the time (the equation of a nation with one cuisine, the hierarchy of cuisines with French above and British below, the emphasis on Paris, the largest French city, as the heart of French cuisine) provide a rich arena within which to try to understand the power of place in the bourgeois imagination. The bourgeois view of the differences between Britain and France, which in the realm of cuisine gave Britain all the defects and France most of the virtues, had a dramatic effect on culinary production and consumption in Britain. And, as we have seen in travel essays, diners' guides, and cookbooks, the authors' attempts to articulate ideas about the nature and substance of British identity and British culinary aptitudes veered between the poles of moral rectitude and artistry and indulgence.[45]

5 APOSTLES OF HAUTENESS

The dominance of French cuisine was well established by the early 1900s, as an item in *The Epicure* from 1903 attests:

An eloquent chef who manages one of those ancient Parisian restaurants where you go for a perfect dinner, and do not trouble about the price, said, in a recent interview, that it was absurd to talk about "French" cookery. All cookery was French. So-called German, English cookery was not cookery at all. There only existed one "cuisine"—*la cuisine*—invented by France. He had read somewhere about the improvements effected in London restaurants of late years, and that it was possible nowadays to dine, not merely to eat, there. But how had London revolutionized its restaurants? Not, he supposed, by attempting to train English cooks. Nor, he imagined, by appointing sons of the fatherland to superintend the kitchen. He had yet to be told of a first-rate London restaurant in which the cooks were not one and all Frenchmen. He would cite another case in point. Take the *menu* of any official dinner in any country in the world. Was it ever anything but French? No; rest assured that as long as the human species continues to live to dine, and not to feed like animals, *la cuisine Française* will reign supreme, for the simple reason that there is no other. Here spoke the chef who began as a kitchen boy and had all his life long had his little world bounded by the walls of a kitchen.[1]

Much is revealed in this story about the eloquent chef. The fact of the ubiquitousness of French cuisine in the public sphere is affirmed, and the reach of the cuisine appears to extend beyond England. He asserts that "official"—which can be read to incorporate courtly, state, and colonial—dinners anywhere have French menus. French cuisine clearly had the global reach its apostle so confidently asserts in urban centers. In the late nineteenth century there were French chefs in such diverse locales as Rome, St. Petersburg, Sydney, and New York. And he is right about the broad reach of French chefs into officialdom. For example, in Rome the Italian court employed French chefs, as did the ambassadors from Austria-Hungary, the United States, and Russia.[2]

The eloquent chef's articulation of French cuisine has the authoritative and dismissive tone of an imperial ruler. His presumed high vantage point is revealed in the comments that this combination of culinary knowledge and practice cannot be understood merely in terms of time and place; transcendent, all-powerful, it is *the* cuisine. Continuing in the same imperialist manner, the chef denies the German and English nations access to cuisine. In his characterization, the English and Germans have access to some type of nourishment, but the manner of preparation precludes any transformation into something as sophisticated as cuisine. On his line of argument, their lack of cuisine also disallows the Germans and English any capacity to "dine." Their consumption practices, it is implied, are of a simpler hand-to-mouth variety.

These comments are highly reminiscent of late nineteenth-century colonial characterizations of the natives as savages who do not possess their own culture and civilization. The chef is speaking, however, of people who in other contexts (including the colonial) were equals and neighbors, not subordinates and "barbarians." With his boasts we begin to see some of the contradictions involved in French culinary imperialism.

At the same time, we see the infiltration of idioms of rule and conquest into the rhetoric of all Europeans during the Age of Empire, even if the observer may be seen by some as merely an *ouvrier* (worker). There is an inherent tension between the imperial manner and the social position of the nineteenth-century French chef. The words of the eloquent chef make it apparent that during this period "imperialism" as a mechanism for acquiring and explaining power was appropriated by many Europeans, and this appropriation happened in locales seemingly remote in both time and space from actual European imperial rule. Throughout this period, French chefs were able to argue for the superiority and necessity of their labor by using the socially explicable idiom of imperialism.[3]

Beyond the chef's sweeping assertions about the power of French cuisine, his insistence on the limits to proper French culinary production is fascinating. The cuisine must be maintained by a ruling cadre of chefs who themselves are French. His view of what type of person is capable of being a master of haute cuisine—a Frenchman—reveals complicity between producers and consumers of French haute cuisine. The complicity involves a mutual commitment to an essentialized category of person in the determination of what it takes to be a master. As seen in the discussions of French cuisine by the English—"we [the British] cannot compare as a nation with France in the science of preparing our daily food"—resorting to cultural nationalism in order to explain individual and group abilities was a type of analysis characteristic of this period. The ability to master French cuisine, which in another time or place could have been analyzed in terms of having the right noble patron or sufficient technical proficiency, during this time of high nationalism was understood to require particular national origins. As the editor of *Food and Cookery and the Catering World* said in 1904, "We have had ample evidence that the Englishman makes an excellent administrator, and if he could only combine his administrative ability with the Frenchman's genius for cooking he would make a first rate chef."[4] Or, in the words of one of his French contemporaries, "Cuisine is an art. It is also an art that is eminently French, in a double sense: The first is that nowhere else has it ever attained the level of refinement as in the homeland of Vatel and Brillat-Savarin; and the second is that almost everywhere (in the civilized countries), the scepter is generally held in the hands of Frenchmen."[5]

The reasons why these producers and consumers were equally committed to the necessity of a French chef and French haute cuisine, however, were highly divergent. Despite the grand words of the eloquent chef, the life of French chefs was not elegant. Their daily practice was physically extremely demanding, and the fact that this practice was understood as a type of manual labor meant their social status was quite low. In fact, in light of the position cooks had in society, the imperial manner of the eloquent chef can be seen as a form of false advertising in the mode proper to the Belle Epoque. Perhaps chefs were invested in the constant and consistent broadcast of the superiority of French cuisine because of the very real limits of their rule.

Chefs: Subalterns and Imperialists?

The maintenance of power is a constant problem for any regime, particularly if the sites of power were as far-flung as they were for French chefs. It has been pointed out in other contexts that an evangelical and disciplining approach to knowledge is an important strategy for successful rule.[6] As we have seen previously, such an approach has a long history in France, including cuisine but also extending beyond it. In fact, the power of other cultural productions is often used by the French who are involved with food to bolster their own rights to power. The chef Antoine Beauvilliers in his 1814 cookbook *L'Art du Cuisinier* states: "The French are honored to have their taste and cuisine reign, in the same imperial manner as their language and their fashion, among all the opulent states of Europe, from the North to the South."[7] Eighty years later, another chef says much the same thing, but, befitting the many political changes of the intervening decades, using more nationalistic language. In 1902 Philéas Gilbert, in a short piece in *L'Art Culinaire*, says: "I can repeat here, and rightly so, the axiom of a great scholar: *France is the mother land of the art of eating: her cuisine and her wines are the pinnacle of gastronomy.*"[8] Cultural nationalism functioned well in the evangelical agendas of French chefs: their audience of bourgeois consumers easily understood the links being made between France, French cultural power, and culinary excellence.

The resistance of subordinated groups to colonial and imperial rule can provide insights to the case of French chefs and the consumers of their cuisine.[9] Ranajit Guha argues that the historiography of imperialism and nationalism has concentrated on elite activities, creating an implicit assumption that nonelites were either passively following the dictates of the elite or not involved in political activities whatsoever. He argues that there was an "autonomous domain" where the "politics of the people" could be found, and to redress this imbalance, the voices of the subaltern classes need to be studied, and their desires for power need to be brought to the forefront of historical analysis.[10] The case of chefs, who in terms of the status of their labor in the context of the emerging capitalist economy and class-based society would have to be understood as both imperialists and subalterns, complicates Guha's argument as to the autonomy of the subaltern domain because in their labor for elites these subalterns used the language of rule to articulate and justify their practice. Also, they were extremely interested in appropriating elite status for themselves. And in the case of the chefs' particular "rule," the people they were colonizing were in other contexts elites.

The voices of the elite commentators and consumers of French cuisine, particularly in outlying "colonies" such as Britain and America, do not reveal much desire for outright rebellion, but notes of ambivalence and irony are sometimes sounded. An example is found in *The Epicure*, a nineteenth-century American journal "Dedicated to the homes of New England in the Interest of Good Living," published by S. S. Pierce. In an article entitled "The Art of the Paris Chef," the author, who had gone to Paris for a culinary exhibition, states:

Someone has said that art is one of the industries in France, and it is just as true that cooking with the French is an art and an industry.... *They take themselves very seriously, these cooks*, and have a great respect for the art of cooking that is very impressive. *Thanks to this attitude of theirs French cookery has been kept up to its present high standard*, and that is why there is no prospect of its lapsing from its position.[11]

The author has mixed feelings about French chefs and their "attitude": it makes them powerful, perhaps skilled, but not very friendly. The essential quality of French cuisine and French chefs is neither denied nor protested against by this author, but considered with a certain ironic detachment, as in the next sentence of the article: "Consequently, it is easy to see why the Paris chef is *sui generis*." Culinary ambivalence can be seen as a strategy of resistance, a type of critique, in the face of the evangelical nature of these French chefs.

The confident words of French chefs must be taken with a grain of salt, however. They needed consumers to believe in the superior cuisine of France, because it was their chance to enter the elite domains of their customers since "people are more aware of tangible class differences than of illusory similarities, more aware of their disadvantages compared with wealthier contemporaries than of their advantages over their ancestors.[12] The public face of the French chef may have been that of a monarch, assured of a long reign, but perhaps it was more the facade of a politician, secretly afraid of losing both his livelihood and his constituency.

French chefs certainly agreed with the bourgeois consumer as to what type of food to make, but they were less in agreement about their own identity and status. Escoffier discusses this issue in his memoirs, as he reminisces about the period of his career from 1860 to 1895, before he became a famous figure: "During this period, the métier of cook or chef was not well regarded in world society. However, that should not be the case, because cooking is a science and an art, and a man who puts all his heart into the task of attaining true talent should be well considered."[13] Cultural values throughout Europe (or, if Escoffier's claims are true, the globe), which easily conceded to the superiority of French cuisine, did not necessarily reflect a social reality rewarding the producers of this superior cuisine with the benefits of political and economic power.

Personal and Occupational Backgrounds

Certain generalizations can be made about the personal histories of French chefs.[14] Usually, these men were born and raised in the French provinces. Their education and induction into the culinary profession came from apprenticeships, which they began between thirteen and sixteen years of age. Some came from families already involved in the food trades; both Pierre Lacam, author of *Le Mémorial Historique et Géographique de la Pâtisserie* (1903), and Jules Gouffé, author of *Le Livre de Cuisine* (1867), came from families who owned pastry shops in provincial towns. But just as many came from families involved in other types of manual labor.

Regardless of place of origin, if a young boy was ambitious he needed to do his apprenticeship in a large town, ideally in Paris. Joseph Favre's occupational biography illuminates the continuities and changes in the culture of work for a chef in France. His life (1849–1903) spanned the second half of the nineteenth century, and by the end of his career he was well known not only as a great chef but also as a tireless organizer on behalf of the profession.

Favre was born in Vex (or Valais) in eastern France and was orphaned quite young. He was raised and educated by a lawyer in his hometown. Though Favre indicated some desire to become a doctor, he was told (given his humble background) that his choices were the priesthood and a *métier manuel* (manual craft), and at fourteen he was sent to a noble home in Sion, the capital of Valais, to be an apprentice cook.[15] After the required three years of apprenticeship, he went to Geneva, where he worked in the Hôtel Métropole. While in Geneva he reportedly took science classes at the university.[16] He was also interested in becoming a master in his profession, so in 1866 he went to Paris to work. In Paris he moved from place to place, usual behavior for chefs in the early days after their apprenticeship. He worked for Chevet, the renowned traiteur and caterer in Paris, and also at another shop of Chevet's in Wiesbaden. By 1870, satisfied that he had become a master of French haute cuisine, he returned to Geneva to take science and nutrition courses at the university.[17] After three years in Geneva, he spent the rest of the decade working in noble homes or grand hotels in Germany, Italy, Britain, and France.

The last twenty years of Favre's career were dedicated to the promotion and elevation of the culinary profession. For years he worked on the book *Dictionnaire Universel de Cuisine Pratique: Encyclopédie Illustrée d'Hygiène Alimentaire*, ultimately published in 1894 with "more than 6,000 recipes, 4 colorized pictures, and 2,000 engravings." He also published the journal *La Cuisine Française et Etrangère* and founded the association Union Universelle pour le Progrès de l'Art Culinaire.

Favre's biography is instructive. His early years are highly typical of other men in the culinary field—the early apprenticeship, the travel from one metropolitan center to another throughout Europe, the gradual movement up the hierarchy of the kitchen. As the century progressed, Favre's career became more unusual because he turned to writing and organizational work. As will become clear in the next chapter, the latter part of his career, with his change in emphasis from the personal mastery of culinary skill to the organization of the culinary profession at large, reflects major shifts in the culture of work among French chefs in the last quarter of the century.

Artisan Life Before 1870

What was the world of work like for members of the *métiers manuels* more generally during the first seventy years of the century? France made a slower transition to an industrialized, capitalist economy than its English-speaking neighbor, and "for much of the nineteenth century old and new economic forms existed side by side." The persistence of an artisanal labor force, which was quite large because by 1848 "only a quarter of all workers were employed in factories," is an example of these simultaneous economic forms.[18]

The typical nineteenth-century artisan was trained as in earlier periods, qualifying for his métier only after a difficult apprenticeship. Many trades—printer, cabinet-maker, carpenter, tailor, hat-maker, for example, all trades of the craftsman—remained immune from the switch to industrialized production.[19] France's slow and episodic move to a capitalist economy meant that ascribed status continued to be a vital factor in decisions about the types of work available to a young man long after the Revolution. And beyond rudimentary schooling, acquisition of knowledge in the artisanal trades was attained "on-site," under the tutelage of a master.

Despite the abolishment of the guild system by legal doctrine in 1791, apprenticeship remained the required method of training in numerous artisanal trades throughout the nineteenth century. It was widely understood that under the apprenticeship tradition young boys in training were not to be paid, and in fact they were often supposed to pay their masters for the privilege of tutelage. With the breakdown of the guild system for all trades, however, the apprenticeship tradition was in constant flux. From 1800 through the 1840s, *compagnonnages*, secret organizations more interested in ritual and social comradery than in prescribing standards of work, are thought to have in some sense replaced the guild structure of the ancien régime.[20] There is no clear evidence of a compagnonnage system for cooks, but there is plenty of evidence that apprenticeship remained the accepted method for training cooks long after the abolishment of guilds.

Labor historians argue that in the case of many trades the apprenticeship tradition was highly compromised not only by the demise of the guilds, but also by the increasing industrialization of manufacture. Leora Auslander, however, questions this directly causal argument and argues that the shift from one organization of production was not so dramatic. Many problems of exploitation were seen under the guild system, and not all aspects of artisanal manufacture went immediately into factory production.[21] She notes that "given the relative low level of mechanization of the furniture trades," it does not appear that industrialization was the cause of the gradual demise of the guild system.

This analysis holds for cooks and chefs. Their labor could never be taken over by machines, and the apprenticeship tradition continued in full force through the nineteenth century and beyond. Just as Auslander documents for French furniture trades, the institutions, associations, and ideas about adequate transmission of knowledge underwent great changes during this period, but their labor continued to be artisanal in nature, and the master-apprentice system remained the paramount method of socialization and training. Some types of foodstuffs, such as bottled food and biscuits, were produced in factory settings by the late 1800s. These products were often used in professional kitchens, but the work of creating complete fine dining meals remained in the hands of trained artisans.

In fact, despite the encroachment of mechanization in France, artisans never lacked a cohesive group identity based on labor practice. The models for the organization of production in the *métiers manuels*, at least in the artisanal trades, which because of their particular type of labor were more resistant to industrialization, show a remarkable resilience during a period in French history otherwise characterized by great turmoil. Much of the turmoil was a product of shifts in the political regime during this period—from monarchy to republic to empire and back to republic. The various regimes had different attitudes toward manual laborers, and manual laborers differed in their attitudes to the various regimes as well. Under the First Republic, for example, the Sociétés de Secours Mutuels, a type of worker's association, were open to qualified members of the public, though they had to be presided over by a police superintendent or mayor and limits were put on membership. These were primarily charitable associations whose mandate was to raise money to aid old, sick, or disabled fellow workers. Sometimes, however, these groups took on more active roles in society, for example in defending workers' rights. By 1834, a workers' uprising caused Louis Philippe's government to augment the Penal Code, as Georges Dupeux has noted: "This law did not destroy all worker's societies but it changed the conditions in which they had to work and replaced informal tolerance by a more arbitrary attitude. Even if the government permitted the foundation of such societies, that permission could always be revoked, and in fact was only extended to those that seemed least offensive."[22] By 1868 the increased prosperity of France enabled the government to develop a fairly benign relationship with workers' societies. The fall of the Second Empire in 1870 signaled the beginning of a new era in the relationship between the French government and the organization of production. There was less suppression of attempts to organize by workers and more knowledge and methods available for workers who wanted to organize. Despite the various attempts at suppression and changes in the relative power of workers' groups, the mutual aid societies persisted.

From the 1870s through the 1890s, workers in the food trades were actively involved in the organization of mutual aid societies and unions, or *chambres syndicales*. They were a part of a larger movement among people involved in *petit commerce*, particularly in Paris, who found it beneficial to organize in the face of threats from emerging big businesses (for example, department stores) and the increasing industrialization of manufacture.[23]

The Apprenticeship

One aspect of the organization of artisans that remained remarkably constant from the ancien régime through the Belle Epoque was apprenticeship as a method of education and induction. Thus, just as before the Revolution, once a boy decided to become a cook he had to go somewhere and apprentice to learn the trade. However, unlike the eighteenth-century pattern, when haute cuisine was being produced only in the courtly sphere, a new commercial public sphere and its new institutions—restaurants, clubs, and hotels—provided more locales to attain culinary expertise.

For a young boy from the provinces with a certain amount of ambition but few connections and little money, the ideal place to go to train was Paris.[24] Paris had the greatest concentration of restaurants, hotels, and cafés where a boy could find a suitable master chef to work under. Just as important, Paris was also a mecca for wealthy dignitaries and nobles who ran large households, entertained grandly, and employed chefs. When it came to elite entertainment, the courtly sphere and the public sphere had parallel lives during the nineteenth century. Historians of France emphasize the dramatic break in the organization of society after the French Revolution, including the demise of the aristocracy and the rise of the bourgeoisie. But the nobility continued to hold tremendous social and cultural power. Dupeux states: "Other social groups looked towards them [the aristocracy] and regarded them as a kind of model to follow."[25] Much of the French aristocracy may have fled France immediately after the Revolution, but as the century wore on many returned. Political upheavals in all countries of Europe continued during the nineteenth century, and Paris became the home (or *a* home) for the nobility of numerous European nations. Many men who became well-known culinary figures in the 1880s and 1890s began their careers during the 1850s and 1860s in these aristocrats' homes.[26]

It is difficult to find first-person accounts of the experiences of apprentices in kitchens during this era. The general sense one derives from the few existing accounts of apprenticeship written by chefs is that it was a period of intense, back-breaking, and often monotonous labor, but that much was learned through observation and the occasional chance to put their own hand to a dish. Gabriel Tschumi discusses his apprenticeship in Queen Victoria's royal kitchen:

> I spent a good deal of my time watching how things were done, working for a fortnight at a time with the various departmental chefs. As meat was eaten in enormous quantities, my spell with the two roast chefs was a good preparation for a fuller study of cuisine. I worked with them before the huge coal ranges which roared away at either end of the Buckingham Palace kitchens, learning the finer points of basting and roasting on a spit.... It was some years before I attempted elaborate dishes at the Palace, and in the early stages, while I was learning, I spoiled a good deal of food. If it was eatable it was given to the staff or to one of the charitable organizations who called regularly collecting food for the poor.[27]

After the apprenticeship was over, there was no consistent method for moving on to a paid position. Often people were kept on at the place where they had their apprenticeship, as is the case with Tschumi, who stayed at the palace, slowly working his way up the kitchen hierarchy, and leaving only in 1932.[28] Just as often, in the early years of their career people moved from job to job, to continue acquiring new skills.

When memoirs are found, the continuity in the training experience from one century to the next is striking. In his memoir, *A Chef's Tale*,

Pierre Franey, a French chef who came to America in the late 1930s and was a chef at the renowned Le Pavillon restaurant in New York City, discusses his apprenticeship at the restaurants Thenin and Drouant in Paris. At the age of fourteen, Franey traveled to Paris from St. Vinnemer in Burgundy, where his father was a blacksmith. For Franey, his apprenticeship was "hard and unwavering," but invaluable because he was "handed over to a subculture of cooks and restaurateurs to be completely imbued with their values and sensibilities, to learn every one of the requisite skills through on-the-job tutelage and endless practice."[29] Franey began his three-year apprenticeship at Restaurant Drouant at the vegetable station. He tells a wonderful story about the importance of skill and stamina to his slow movement up the kitchen hierarchy:

> The tyrant Domas [a sous-chef] came to the vegetable station and said: . . . "Mignon, today you are going to make omelettes." If he hadn't felt the need to stand over me as the first order came in, everything would have been wonderful, I'm sure of it. I was told to prepare a simple omelette aux fines herbes—three eggs, chervil, parsley, tarragon, chives—the very first omelette I was assigned to prepare for paying guests, after considerable amount of practice on others. I knew what I was doing. I chopped the herbs rapidly, broke and mixed the eggs with the herbs, poured the mixture into the heated pan.[30]

Here was where Franey could show his mastery of important skills. For the French, the signs of a perfectly cooked omelette are fluffiness and a perfectly smooth exterior when turned out of the pan, "like a baby's bottom" it is often said. But there was a problem with Franey's omelette.

> It was wrinkled. The skinny dictator Domas seethed with scorn. "That's no omelette aux fines herbes, that's an omelette grand-mère!" he said in an allusion to the wrinkles. He whacked the side of my head with his spatula. I took that malformed omelette and hurled it at his face; it struck its target, and pieces of egg, as if in slow motion, gradually broke away, slipping down the front of his body. I spun around and sped up the stairs, three flights.[31]

Domas was in fact impressed with Franey's performance; Franey completed his apprenticeship and went on to become a famous chef and cookbook author in America.

In *Down and Out in Paris and London*, George Orwell documents his journeys into working-class life in London and Paris during the late 1920s. Though of a later era than this study, Orwell's descriptions of the large hotel kitchen he worked in as a plongeur, or dishwasher, eloquently portray a physical and social environment much like the ones where young French boys worked during the latter part of the nineteenth century. Orwell calls his place of employment the Hotel X., and given his descriptions of it as a "vast, grandiose place" that was "one of the dozen most expensive hotels in Paris," it was probably among the many hotels (such as the Ritz) that were built in Paris during the 1880s.

One of the less alluring sides of being in the production rather than the consumption side of public fine dining was that much less money was put into the building and maintenance of service areas. The diner at a grand hotel would be treated to elaborate carpets, beveled mirrors, candelabra, and fine dinnerware. In contrast, here is Orwell's description the kitchen of Hotel X.:

> The kitchen was like nothing I had ever seen or imagined—a stifling, low-ceilinged inferno of a cellar, red-clanging of pots and pans. It was so hot that all the metal-work except the stoves had to be covered with cloth. In the middle were furnaces, where twelve cooks skipped to and fro, their faces dripping with sweat in spite of their white caps. Round that were counters where a mob of waiters and *plongeurs* clamoured with trays. Scullions, naked to the waist, were stoking the fires and scouring huge copper saucepans with sand.[32]

That this was a description of the norm is confirmed by Gabriel Tschumi's comments on the high quality of the royal kitchens compared to those of London hotels of the late nineteenth and early twentieth centuries. Tschumi talks of how impressed he was that in the royal kitchens the equipment was new and clean, and recalls that the kitchen reminded him "of a chapel with its high domed ceiling" and "its feeling of airiness and light."[33]

During his ten-week stint in the kitchens of Hotel X., Orwell took notice of another striking aspect of the professional kitchen as a workplace—the rigid and extremely hierarchical division of labor. First, there was a consistent and often divisive separation between the "front of the house" (the manager, the maître d'hôtel, the waiters) and the "back" or the kitchen (the chef de cuisine, the cooks and bakers, the apprentices, the scullions, and the dishwashers). Orwell calls it a caste system: "Our staff, amounting to about a hundred and ten, had their prestige graded as accurately as that of soldiers, and a cook or waiter was as much above a plongeur as captain above a private."[34] Orwell characterizes hotel work, especially at the lowest level where he was laboring, as tedious and oppressive, but interestingly, he has kinder words for cooks and their practice.

> Undoubtably the most workmanlike class, and the least servile, are the cooks. They do not earn quite so much as waiters, but their prestige is higher and their employment steadier. The cook does not look upon himself as a servant, but as a skilled workman; he is generally called "un ouvrier," which a waiter never is. He knows his power—knows that he alone makes or mars a restaurant, and that if he is five minutes late everything is out of gear. . . . And he takes a genuine artistic pride in his work, which demands very great skill.[35]

Orwell's observations of the hotel kitchen remain accurate today. A tour of the kitchens of London's Savoy Hotel in 1987 left me with the same impressions. Shunted off into the basement, the "kitchen" was in fact a rabbit's warren of small rooms with little or no ventilation. Even on a cool day, the heat was tremendous in the main kitchen. Work stations were separated by long, dark, narrow hallways, and workers were constantly running to and fro from room to room to get their work done. Today's professional chefs think themselves lucky if they work in a kitchen with a window that affords them natural light and enough space for every cook to have a separate work station.

Changes in Educational Norms

Orwell's discussion of cooks as skilled workers rather than mere servants also reveals the inherent tensions of the role and status of cooking and cooks in larger institutions like the hotel. The labor of the chef during the nineteenth century could be understood in terms of service (in both patronage and commercial senses) and artisanry (as both worker and artist) against the backdrop of the demise and obsolescence of the older institutional structures of the guild and patronage and the slow transformation of the economy. Understandings of training, identity, and status were always changing.

Education thus became of increasing concern to members of the French artisanal class. The French state addressed the issue of state-sponsored education by enacting a number of laws, among them an 1850 law that made primary education for boys mandatory in communes of 800 inhabitants or more. By 1882 a law was in place mandating free primary education, and another that required primary education for both boys and girls between the ages of six and thirteen.[36] The rights to a primary education came to be considered a right of all French citizens.

Access to education and educational degrees also became increasingly linked to the proper acquisition of occupational skills.

By the 1850s the higher education system in France had become more complex than the pre-Revolutionary model of a very few elite collèges, écoles, and académies. In a report, *Les Consommations de Paris*, Armand Husson, a member of the Institut de l'Académie de Médecine, provided the following list of establishments of higher or professional education as of 1869:

> Ecole de droit; Ecole de Médecine; Ecole de Pharmacie; Ecole Polytechnique; Ecole de Ponts et Chaussées; Ecole des Mines; Ecole d'Etat-Major; Ecole Normale Supérieure; Ecole des Chartes; Séminaire des Saint-Sulpices; Ecole des Beaux-Arts; Conservatoire de Musique et Déclamation Dramatique; Ecole Supérieure du Commerce; Ecole Centrale des Arts et Manufactures; Ecole Commerciale; Ecole de Musique Religieuse; Ecole d'Accouchement pour les Sages Femmes.[37]

By that time some of the new schools provided technical rather than artistic, religious, or scientific training. The Ecole de Ponts et Chaussées, Ecole des Mines, Ecole des Chartes, Ecole Commerciale, and Ecole Centrale des Arts et Manufactures all offered higher education that would train people whose function was to provide services involving the new technologies that were part of industrialization in France. Cooking, not a readily mechanized form of labor, did not fit easily into the new educational system, whose curriculum relied heavily on mastering abstract scientific information. No school for training people in the food trades was a part of this first wave of technical schools in France.

French Chefs as Artisans Abroad

Job opportunities abroad made the culinary profession highly unusual in light of its status as a métier manuel during the nineteenth century. The demand for French haute cuisine by the aristocracy and bourgeoisie, and the widely accepted view that only the French could produce true haute cuisine, meant that young chefs could easily find employment outside France. In fact, many biographies of chefs include substantial periods, sometimes entire careers, spent abroad. Alfred Suzanne, born in 1829 in Normandy, left France in 1847 to work in the kitchens of the earl of Clarendon, the lord-lieutenant of Ireland. He spent the subsequent forty years in Ireland and England, working also for the earl of Wilton and the duke of Bedford, until he retired to France in 1887.[38] Charles

Figure 5. Two examples of chef's uniforms, one typical of the Second Empire (left), the other of the Third Republic. Schlesinger Library, Radcliffe College.

Figure 6. The Chef. Courtesy of Barbara Ketcham Wheaton.

Dietrich, born in Lorraine, began as an apprentice at the Café Riche in Paris. He then moved to Rome, where he found continuous employment for over twenty years, including a ten-year stint as chef de cuisine for the United States Ambassador to Rome.[39] During a forty-year career that spanned the latter half of the century, Joseph Favre worked in Switzerland, Germany, France, and England, in all the institutions that required professional chefs: restaurants, hotels, and noble homes.[40] Given the long and proficient careers of such figures as Suzanne, Dietrich, and Favre, it is no wonder that the bourgeois consumer thought fancy food was French, for the French were everywhere.

Chefs and the Changing Culture of Work After 1870

The food trades retained many of their pre-Revolutionary characteristics throughout the century: dependence on consumer patronage, education via apprenticeship, and small-scale production. By 1870, however, workers had realized that the culture of work was changing dramatically in European society at large. In the 1860s, in reaction to such changes, people involved with what were traditionally called the *métiers d'alimentation*—cuisiniers, chefs de cuisine, pâtissiers, boulangers, traiteurs — started to organize. These organized groups were not initially state sanctioned institutions as the guilds had been, but many of their struggles were to create a regulated and supported system of practice that could function in the same way.

This phase in the organization of food production has many characteristics typical of community building and worker movements in France during the Third Republic (1870–1914). Philip Nord, who has investigated the organizing efforts of small shopkeepers in Paris during the Third Republic, argues that fear of increasingly large-scale operations producing similar goods and services compelled those involved in smaller operations to join together.

> The eleven *chambres syndicales* of the Comité de l'alimentation took out membership en masse at this junction [the 1880s and 1890s], followed by associations, sometimes more than one to a profession. The ligue syndicale movement was in large part an outgrowth of the chambre syndicale movement, but—and this is the second point—its capacity to draw on already existing retailer organizations for support was limited to certain trades and did not extend to others. *Food and drink men, retailers of luxury goods, and clothing merchants proved most responsive to the appeal of small shopkeeper defence.*[41]

An example of a change in the organization of production that was of great concern to "food and drink men" was the development of food processing plants. Félix Potin started a plant outside Paris in 1859 that employed almost two thousand people by 1900.[42] Nord also discusses the fate of those involved in food manufacture combined with the retail of food.

> The improvement of the Paris transport system made possible the emergence of large suburban dairies which rapidly won a monopoly on the production of milk, reducing the milkman to the status of a simple retailer. Charcutiers and tripiers experienced a similar transformation. Curing factories, which could mass produce smoked hams, salt pork and sausage at minimum expense turned pork butchering into a large-scale industrial enterprise.[43]

Defining group boundaries and adequately addressing their needs also became a pressing issue to workers in an era where identity was no longer confined to local institutions. This was of particular concern to French cuisiniers, pâtissiers, and chefs de cuisine because their geographic spread was so vast.

Associations and Journals: The Dissemination of a New Culture

Men involved in organizing thus used two new resources: associations and journals. In the period between 1860 and 1900, more than ten new associations and ten new journals involved with food were founded in Paris alone.[44] Often a journal was the official organ of one of the associations. From the start of this phase of the organization of production in the food trades of France, particularly with the cuisiniers and pâtissiers, organization also involved locales outside France. The Union Universelle pour le Progrès de l'Art Culinaire, founded in 1879, had "more than 24 branches in all parts of the world, including San Francisco, New York, Odessa, Madrid, Turin, Milan, Saint Petersburg, and London."[45] The Société des Cuisiniers had a large branch in London. The journal L'Art Culinaire had subscribers in Algeria and America, as did the more politically oriented Progrès des Cuisiniers. The fact that the associations founded in Paris during this period were directed to colleagues in such far-flung locales points to an ongoing dialectic between the structural constraints and the imperial attitudes of French chefs. Their economic and political reign was always tenuous. By creating a structure of associations that resembled an octopus with Paris as the head, French chefs, who were always at the center of these associations, could control the dissemination of professional knowledge and keep French haute cuisine at the forefront. Thus two themes recur constantly in the agendas of the associations and journals: to preserve and promote the power and integrity of French haute cuisine and to elevate the status of the profession.

Technological and social changes during the nineteenth century allowed for the rapid rise of book, newspaper, and periodical publication in Europe, which in turn helped solidify the power of French haute cuisine. The invention of the steam-powered cylinder press in 1814 greatly increased the speed of print production: between 1814 and 1830, output went from 250 to 8,000 sheets per hour. The production of wood-pulp paper began in 1843. By the 1880s, Linotype presses, which removed the necessity of copy being set by hand, were vital to newsprint production. All these technological inventions fostered a precipitous rise in the number and circulation of books, periodicals, and newspapers. In the early nineteenth century, a leading Parisian daily newspaper had a circulation of 20,000; by 1900 at least four had a circulation of a million.[46]

The French state produced a number of laws that concerned the freedom of press and had divergent effects on newspaper and periodical production. In July 1881, however, a law abolished all restrictions on freedom of the press. The end of state restrictions helped precipitate the expansion of production; for example, in 1880 there were 114 provincial daily papers and by 1885 there were 280.[47]

The most important social change that encouraged the increased production of books, periodicals, and newspapers was the rise of literacy. The development of a more literate public was in part a result of the social and political interest from the 1860s to the 1880s in providing primary education to citizens. In Britain, the Forster Act of 1870 made the government accountable for primary education where voluntary institutions were not available or sufficient.[48] In France, by 1882, school attendance for youths between six and thirteen years of age was made mandatory, and also free. By the late 1880s, the combination of both a larger literate public and a wider array of reading material helped create a new culture of reading in Europe.

These changes had a considerable impact on the smaller arena of culinary publications. From the 1870s on, a whole series of culinary journals founded in France, Britain, and America became a vital part of the dissemination of ideas about cooking in these areas.[49] By tracing the connection between journals, we can see the development of a very organized professional culinary community during the late nineteenth century, primarily in Paris, but also beyond. For example, within a year of its initial publication in France in 1893, *Le Pot au Feu* began to publish an

English language version of the journal, and the Société des Cuisiniers Français had branches in New York and London. Reading the journals they produced, we can learn the preoccupations and agendas of this particular community. Apparent in all the journals is a tremendous focus on the promotion and maintenance of culinary standards, which in this era meant education in the principles and methods of French haute cuisine. During this period, when periodicals at least were financed primarily by subscription, periodicals and newspapers could be much more selective in their aims, since their readers, especially during the period under discussion, had make a long-term commitment: a year, two years, twenty-four issues.

Though the majority of the culinary journals examined were begun in the period 1870–1900, some were started earlier, notably the *Almanach des Gourmands*, written and published in France by Alexandre Grimod de la Reynière from 1804 to 1812. He is considered, with Brillat-Savarin, to be one of the first of the French gastronomes. The definition involves someone who is interested in the art of fine eating but also concerned with the promotion of fine taste to the society at large. Charles Monselet, following in de la Reynière's footsteps, founded (in 1858) and edited *Le Gourmet: Journal des Intérêts Gastronomiques*, a journal devoted primarily to restaurant reviews, poems about food, and wine columns.[50] It appears that French journals until 1870 were written exclusively by and for gastronomes.

The culinary journals from 1870 to 1900 are of a very different tenor, and many more were produced. In this period, in France alone, twelve journals were founded, and in Britain and America at least another ten. These publications, published weekly, bi-monthly, or monthly, were generally not intended for the sophisticated man-about-town, looking for the best restaurant. Broadly speaking, two distinct social groups were in the market for the later culinary journals: women concerned with domestic food preparation and men in professional practice. This division in audience was similar to that for the cookbooks also being produced at the time.

The journals written with a female audience in mind are primarily instructional in organization and format. Never more than sixteen pages in length, they are printed on newsprint, not glossy coated pages, and they do not include advertisements. Layout rarely changes from issue to issue. *Le Pot au Feu*, with its subtitle *Journal de la Cuisine Pratique et d'Economie Domestique*, was a popular journal of this genre. The subscription cost was five francs a year, six francs if it was mailed to the subscriber. In the 1890s each issue begins with a "class" taught by Auguste Colombié or Charles

Driessens, both professional chefs. For example, in the March 15, 1895 issue, Colombié provides a lesson on how to make pluviers dorés en salmis, or ragoût of gilded plover. More than a simple recipe is provided—Colombié gives detailed instructions on how to prepare the bird for roasting and how to make the sauce. This issue also includes other recipes and menus, as well as short articles. Among the articles are a review of the Exposition Culinaire of 1895 and a discussion of the merits of bread baked in a wood-fired oven.

The fact of Colombié's participation in this journal aimed primarily at housewives deserves further discussion. Colombié was a major culinary figure in Paris at the time. He provided cooking lessons in a similar women's journal of the era, *Le Gourmet*, he conducted cooking classes, and he published several books. The books were a compilation of the cooking lectures and were aimed at the same audience as the journals—bourgeois women.[51] Colombié is just one of many professional male chefs who were vitally involved in the dissemination of "classic" culinary knowledge to the Parisian housewife. Charles Driessens had his own successful cours de cuisine for women, given at the headquarters of the Gas Company, which was surely trying to entice women into accepting the new technology of gas ovens and purchasing them for their households. These male chefs appear to be instrumental in the creation and production of a majority of the journals.

During the same period, journals were being founded to cater to the needs of the culinary profession, which between 1870 and 1900 was growing in size and becoming increasingly organized. These journals were often longer than the women's journals, and the ratio of articles and editorials to recipes was greater. Their appearance was strikingly similar, however, down to the same format for the *sommaire*, or table of contents, on the first page.

Some of this similarity arises from the fact that the same people were writing in both of them. Charles Driessens also wrote articles for *L'Art Culinaire*, the leading professional journal of the day. F. Barthélemy, a contributor to *L'Art Culinaire*, was for a time editor-in-chief of *Le Cordon Bleu* magazine, and it was the initial success of the latter as an instructional journal that led to the subsequent founding of the school Le Cordon Bleu by Marthe Distel. Yearly culinary expositions, which were founded by the Société des Cuisiniers Français to promote the art of French cuisine and raise money, included the work of Colombié's and Driessen's female students. At the Exposition of 1895, fifty of Driessens's students prepared, in public, the same luncheon menu, which a reviewer in *Le Pot au Feu* characterized as "competent and wholesome."[52]

The professional journals address a more diverse array of topics related to the food practices and values of the day. For example, *L'Art Culinaire*, founded in 1883 as the journal of the Société des Cuisiniers Français, was explicitly and solely directed toward public practitioners of the craft. The cost of subscription was twelve francs a year, with subscribers as far away as America and Algeria. Menus and recipes were included in every bimonthly issue, but the bulk of the writing is devoted to concerns of the profession. Articles covered issues like the importance of apprenticeship, the need to found a school for professional training, and the numerous ways cooking can be understood as both an art and a science.

We see the same overlap of information, preoccupations, and participants in *L'Art Culinaire* as we see in the women's magazines. The July 1885 issue had two articles on the importance of professional instruction in French cuisine, devoted to the relative merits of providing basic cooking classes to housewives and the other to the necessity of convincing the state to support a school for male chefs.

L'Art Culinaire's editorial board knew exactly whom they wanted to captivate and influence: professional male chefs. And the editors of *Le Pot au Feu*, *Le Gourmet*, and *Le Cordon Bleu* knowingly concerned themselves with another community: urban bourgeois housewives and their female domestic servants. With specific aims for their more captive audience, these journals provide more explicit information on culinary values and practices than a cookbook. By simply examining a cookbook, even for example Colombié's *Traité Pratique de Cuisine Bourgeoise*, we would not know that the women taking his classes were not only visiting, but also participating in the grand public spectacle of classic French cuisine of the time: the culinary exposition. These journals created an "imagined community" of like-minded readers, some in search of a social identity, some in search of a professional identity. And what unified all these readers was a dedication to a particular type of cooking, and a particular form of cuisine.[53]

French chefs of this era had many of the same occupational struggles as their fellow artisans. In particular, they were united with other groups, such as those in the furniture trades, in their concerns about the encroachment of industrialization, the increasing stratification of French society along class lines, and the loss of their status as craftsmen and artists. However, because of the long-standing reputation of French cuisine outside France, which made them extremely sought after and highly employable internationally, their professional preoccupations were much wider in scope. French chefs simultaneously had to keep their standards and their reputations intact, or their opportunities for social advancement and professional power would disappear, as seen in this comment by a contemporary: "That there is an abundance of skilled French *chefs* to be found in all centres of civilization the whole world over is indubitable, but it would be interesting to learn whether the art once rendered illustrious by Vatel yet flourishes in undiminished excellence on its native soil."[54] If chefs did not hold on to the elite reputation of their craft, they would be condemned to being one of the groups of forgotten craftsmen of the pre-Industrial Age, such as umbrella makers and hatters. The next chapter examines how chefs struggled to maintain their standards and elevate their reputation.

6 SCHOOLS, STANDARDS,

AND STATUS

Raymond Williams's book *The Country and the City* investigates the transformation of the English country and city with the development of a new division of labor in the modern period, which intensified under capitalism. With the growing importance of industrialization and capitalism, he sees an increasing separation "between mental and manual labour, between administration and operation, between politics and social life."[1] Our organization of space and ideas are profoundly altered. Williams maps the myriad consequences of division of labor on every aspect of human existence: the sense of time, of work, of self.

Points of contact can certainly be found in the story of the agency of French chefs in promoting and disseminating a French culinary imperialism. Changes in the division of labor under capitalism affected their practice, and all their organizational activities during the nineteenth century revolve around their status and role in this increasingly demarcated division of labor.

There is no dearth of literature on the division of labor in the West under modernity. Scholars who have focused on capitalism as an economic system, however, have concentrated on ownership of the means of production and access to economic capital as the major dividing force between the bourgeois and working classes. Other forms of "capital" also played a vital role in the particular outcomes of the division of labor, that is, which laboring group ended up being associated with the bourgeoisie and which with the workers. In understanding the eventual place of cooks and chefs in the new hierarchy of labor that emerged in the late nineteenth century, access to what I call "knowledge capital" is as important as access to economic capital.

In order to explore the importance of knowledge capital to the place of cooks and chefs in the division of labor, it is necessary to explore their labor practice. One issue is whether cooking in the modern public sphere can be understood to be a profession, or whether it is better characterized as a trade, manual labor, or artisanal craft. A related question is whether the situation differs for the nineteenth and twentieth centuries. The primary documents on the organization of production reveal the aims and goals of concerned laborers; these men called themselves professionals, but is what they said fact or rhetoric or ideology? Sociologists of the professions cast a wary eye on many groups that purport or purported to be professions. According to those involved in a deductive analysis of chefs' organization and labor, something required for professional status is missing.

Yet the men organizing themselves and writing about their labor in the late 1800s spoke of themselves as professionals and members of the culinary profession. People cooking in the public sphere wanted to be considered professionals, and they worked very hard to obtain the social, political, and economic approbation that would give them this status. At that time, one of their ongoing frustrations was that the larger society was not forthcoming in validating their professional claims. In this they were not alone. The organization of certain occupations into professions in Europe was played out in a field of competing forces. Many groups found the professional model a desirable one to aspire to and organize around, but larger social dynamics of exclusion and inclusion ultimately only allowed a relative few occupations to become understood as legitimate professions in modern capitalist society.

According to Magali Sarfatti Larson, in modern capitalist society group success or failure in the professionalizing process lies in the ability to organize a protected market for its services. The capacity for closure (as in nineteenth-century France, where stonemasons, mechanics, and surveyors were ultimately not defined as "engineers") makes some people professionals and many others laborers. As will become clear, using her criteria, the history of nineteenth-century chef-organizers can be seen as a valiant but ultimately failed attempt to become a profession.

Education, Larson argues, is the primary means of attaining and maintaining the closure necessary for long-term professional success. Her definition is still more precise: higher education is the method to obtain the appropriate expert knowledge that defines professional status. She argues that in fact a primary function of professions is to organize mechanisms to control membership, using certain educational credentials to ascertain the attainment of mastery. Discussions of cooks and chefs are not found in the literature on the sociology of professions: they are a marginal group. The relegation of cooks and chefs to the hinterlands of the professions is the result of a "lack of fit" between cooking as a type of labor and the definition of knowledge and practice within the professional paradigm. Following Larson's definition, the wall that separates chefs from other professions is the nature of their knowledge. Cooking as a mode of "expertise" cannot easily be incorporated into the emerging system of higher education Larson considers axiomatic in the transformation of practice into profession.

Cooking as a practice confounds Larson's dictum because of its sheer ubiquity. Historically, this posed an obvious problem for chefs arguing that their practice involved esoteric knowledge and therefore deserved (in Larson's terms) a "protected market." The everyday reality of cooking as a domestic practice meant their claims for closure were constantly undergoing negation. Also, cooking has traditionally been women's work, and the gendered understanding of this practice created yet another problem for chefs interested in erecting boundaries around their labor. This problem was especially acute in the late nineteenth century because, just as chefs were developing social arguments to justify higher status in their society, the doctrine of "separate spheres" for men and women was becoming increasingly incorporated as an organizational principle into Western social life. Thus, not only was it difficult to separate this practice from the mundane, it was difficult to consider this practice distanced from the domestic sphere. Hence the continued preoccupation of chefs with expensive and hard-to-find ingredients and with dishes that are difficult and time-consuming to prepare—traditional elements of haute cuisine. Also, in the end the results of cooking are ephemeral. This deprived chefs of a product of their labor that would be available for social display and sustained social critique: they had only the moment of consumption to entice and engage the consumer in regard to the excellence of their work.

Despite these hindrances, chefs worked hard to fulfill the conditions for professional status. They formed associations, founded a school that combined practical and theoretical knowledge in its curriculum, held conferences and competitions, and lobbied for state sanction and support. And finally, woven into all these efforts was a consistent claim that their labor required expert knowledge in order to be adequately performed.

Men involved with the organization of culinary production from 1870 to 1910 engaged in all the activities considered necessary to mark themselves as professionals and not workers. Although in a final analysis, from the point of view of contemporary observers, cooking did not become a profession, the attempts of chefs to professionalize were not in vain. Their activities had profound, though unanticipated, long-term effects on societal ideas about their practice.

Profession Versus Trade

It is difficult to delineate the difference, historically, between a trade and a profession, because over time the definitions of the terms have changed. W. J. Reader points out that in eighteenth-century Britain, the term "profession" could signify any "calling, vocation, known employment," and in fact the term "mechanical professions" was frequently used to characterize what would be now understood as skilled labor.[2] With the historian's retrospective gaze, one can see that the occupations which became those that fit the widely understood definition of profession in the 1800s and 1900s were those known in the eighteenth century as the "liberal" occupations. These were occupations that required, as Reader succinctly puts it, "the education of a gentleman, and not of a trader or an artisan."[3] Education in classical Greek and Roman knowledge was the primary mode of differentiation, and such mastery was required of doctors, lawyers, and parsons. These were the acceptable occupations of a gentleman.

Shifts in the terrain of occupational terminology occurred in France as well during the course of the eighteenth and nineteenth centuries. John H. Weiss documents the wide array of people involved in "technological and managerial activities" during this time who could have fallen under the rubric of "engineer"—architects, mechanics, artisans, land surveyors, stonemasons, and so on—but in fact only a certain few were able to take this name. The story of the increased differentiation in this occupational milieu parallels the British situation: it was access to and completion of a liberal education, here completion of the baccalaureate, that ultimately allowed some to call themselves engineers while many others could not.[4]

Terminological shifts reflect a wider social uncertainty as to the classification of labor under capitalism. During the 1880s, Joseph Barberet, the member of the Ministry of Interior under the Third Republic who supervised the various workers' associations such as the Sociétés de Secours Mutuels, published a massive six-volume work, *Monographies Professionnelles*. Covering 250 different occupations, the book today seems to be concerned only with occupations of traders, artisans, and laborers, and not professionals. Barberet considers his book to be the documentation of the "concerns of the working class," and he states: "The most important issues for them are 'les questions professionnelles.' "[5] From the point of view of people deeply involved in the organization of production at that time, these were not contradictory concerns. In a series of articles in *L'Art Culinaire* during 1890 called "Chronique Professionnelle," the author discusses the plight of the cuisinier-ouvrier and his special professional concerns in the same sentence.[6] Also, the state-subsidized school for training boys to be cooks and chefs founded in 1890 was called the L'Ecole Professionnelle de Cuisine.

The development of a training school for an occupation that previously relied solely on informal apprenticeship for the transmission of knowledge was not unique to cuisine. Neither was the official appellation of the school as the *Ecole Professionnelle*. In 1880, the French state passed the Ecoles Manuelles d'Apprentissage law, which gave state sanction to the development of schools to train workers in the manual trades. These schools were locally funded. By 1890, the Conseil Municipal de Paris provided funds for at least nine different trade schools, including l'Ecole Professionnelle d'Ameublement for people in the furniture trades and the Ecole Professionnelle de la Rue Fonday for people involved with the fashion trades.[7] As Leora Auslander points out, "The late 19th century was a transitional period in the definition of responsibility for the training of the young and the control of knowledge in the industrial arts."[8] A generalized manifestation of the shifting definition and status of occupations in this era was an increasing concern that occupational knowledge become formalized and institutionalized via schools. Characterizations of differences and similarities in forms of labor were under constant negotiation. And these changes and negotiations occurred throughout Europe, albeit the historical chronologies of organization varied from country to country.

The nineteenth-century French gloss for "professionnelle" was not so broad that it encompassed what we now see to be two distinct categories in the division of labor—profession and trade—if we take as evidence the writings of chef-organizers. Châtillon-Plessis, who wrote extensively for *L'Art Culinaire* and was heavily involved in the organization of culinary production in the late 1800s, bemoans the characterization of chefs and cuisiniers as "ouvriers" by the state when they were put under the jurisdiction of the Conseil de Prud'hommes in 1889.[9] He says, "The title of ouvrier [worker] recognized by the law does not elevate the cook. All it does is classify him—and this classification is lower than what is desirable."[10] He argues that the classification of cooks as workers has added nothing to the goal of *professional progress* and *professional authority*, and wonders at the fact that pharmacists were not classified as workers but cooks were. Châtillon-Plessis believes "la Cuisine—bien pratique—est un art, non un métier," and so cooks should be understood as artists and intellectuals, not workers. To involved and knowledgeable members of the culinary community, the long-term social ramifications of the definition of cooking as "manual" labor and cooks as workers was clear. Chefs would not be considered professionals and would be deprived of the economic and social approbation they so desired.

Châtillon-Plessis refines his ideas about the organization of the culinary profession further in his book *La Vie à Table à la Fin du XIXème Siècle*. In the chapter "Le Cuisinier" he employs the oft-used refrain "the strongest representatives of France to foreigners are her language and her cuisine," and thus declares it irresponsible of French state and society to neglect the "cuisinier français." He goes on to say that, given French cuisine's worldwide reputation and appeal, chefs, like pharmacists, should be seen in the first or second class. He than admits that not all Frenchmen who work in public kitchens are of that first rank in talent and skill, so a hierarchy within the kitchen should certainly exist: the lower echelons can be called *aides*, another gloss for *ouvrier*.[11]

The struggles of chefs to mark the appropriate occupational territory for the practice between 1870 and 1910 reflect the shifting sands of the division of labor, particularly the gradual parting of mental from manual labor. Although the form of their labor makes their story in many ways unique, some of their struggles also easily fit into larger developments in the organization of production. Until this epoch a vast proportion of the population of Europe did handicraft and agricultural work in rural areas, but with the increase in mechanized and industrial work many people moved to the city and worked for wages. As their labor practices and the social status of their labor changed, so did their labor identity. People began to organize, and they organized around being workers. Like the aspiring professionals, wage laborers attempted to get social, political, and economic approbation for themselves as a group. The organization of groups who considered their labor identity to be that of the "working class" developed rapidly and powerfully between 1880 and 1905.[12]

It has long been considered that what was unusual about the working-class movements of this era was their unity as a class and possession of a "class consciousness," despite internal occupational, regional, and national differences. Socialist organizers and political thinkers of the day envisioned that the power of class solidarity and discontent over labor conditions would propel the working class to rise up and destroy bourgeois capitalist rule. This was a powerful and important aim, but unfortunately it was never realized. The reasons why have been an intellectual preoccupation of many ever since, and there is no simple answer as to the failure of the working class to unite. One problem that resonates with the concerns of those groups involved in the professionalizing process during the same period, however, was contention between (seemingly) closely allied occupational groups. As Eric Hobsbawm puts it: "Industries, crafts, or other occupations, often extremely localized and with the most geographically restricted horizons, did not see their problems and situations as the same. . . . These divisions were not only vertical but horizontal: between craftsmen and laborers, between 'respectable people' and occupations."[13] An overall problem of occupational organization, be it as "workers" or "professionals," was the complexity and contradiction of aims within their supposedly larger solidarities. In the final analysis, among cooks and chefs, the unity they possessed as a community of laborers was their specialized knowledge and expertise: they had solidarity, but it was not solely class solidarity. Their primary work identity was formed around the specifics of their labor practices, or the mastery of their skill. Thus, though chefs, cooks, and other artisans certainly recognized some commonalities, they appear to have fought their battles from within their own territory.

By the 1870s, when people involved with the food trades in France aspired to have their occupational identity defined as a profession and organized accordingly, they were very aware of a model from above (gentlemanly liberal educations) and below (the organization of artisanal trades and workers) as parameters for the development of their labor practice. Implementation of these models was often being used simultaneously. For example, although for purposes of structural and social elevation the professions of the period promoted abstract learning and examinations as the primary means to attain entry into the profession, apprenticeship in fact remained a vital part of the process of becoming a professional up until very recently. Thus, though from an analytic perspective it is possible to see a strong break in what constitutes a profession versus a trade, it may be more important to consider the permeability between the two occupational structures. This is especially the case in a study of the late 1800s, because by this time there was plenty of precedent in European societies for a successful transition to being a profession. As Harold Perkin puts it: "The professional hierarchies . . . reach much further down the social pyramid than ever landlordship or even business capital did, and embrace occupations formerly thought beyond the reach of professional aspiration."[14] Many groups not at that time considered a profession used that model in their own efforts to organize

their occupation within a capitalist economic system and position themselves in these new labor hierarchies.

L'Art Culinaire: *Chef as Professional and Artist*

As discussed in the previous chapter, associations and journals were
vital to the professionalizing process. The journal *L'Art Culinaire*, published from 1883 until the 1920s, was founded originally by a Monsieur
Dancourt, an "homme de lettres," but soon became primarily the official
organ of the Société des Cuisiniers Français. This society was the main
division of the umbrella association, Union Universelle pour le Progrès
de l'Art Culinaire, conceived by Joseph Favre and founded in 1879. Cen-
trally located in Paris, the Société des Cuisiniers Français functioned as
the central clearinghouse for all the other divisions of the Union Universelle, at home and abroad. The journal was published twice a month and
was primarily available by subscription. During its long sojourn, the ad-
ministrators and the writers involved with *L'Art Culinaire* were almost
exclusively professional chefs.

The Société des Cuisiniers Français always had (among an already
highly considered group of artisans) an elite aura, primarily because of
the high status of the founding members, who were all well-known chefs
de cuisine and included Achille Ozanne, Charles Poulain, and Eduard
Capdeville. The association was founded in April 1882 with two clear
aims: to found a professional cooking school and to develop culinary
expositions to promote French haute cuisine and raise money for the
school. The association appears to have been highly organized; the journal was published regularly and the expositions were successful annual
events. For twelve years these men diligently pursued the goal of a professional culinary school. The school was founded but lasted less than
two years. The Société des Cuisiniers Français was disbanded after the
closing of the school, but the journal continued. Meanwhile, two former
members of the Société decided that the culinary expositions should
continue with a new aim: to help create a retirement home for older
workers in the food trades. Thus a new association was founded, the
Union Philanthropique Culinaire et de l'Alimentation.[15] The journal—
L'Art Culinaire—and the Société des Cuisiniers Français counted among
their participants many chefs who remain distinguished to this day. Auguste Escoffier was on the editorial committee of the journal during the
1880s and occasionally submitted recipes. Prosper Montagné, who published cookbooks that included the highly influential *Larousse Gastronomique* and who became a chef-instructor at the Cordon Bleu school

during the early part of the 1900s, wrote articles for the journal. Another writer for *L'Art Culinaire* was Urbain Dubois, renowned in his day (and today) for publishing a series of important books on French haute cuisine.[16] The journal also published articles by men who were journalists and gastronomes though not chefs: Châtillon-Plessis and Fulbert-Dumonteil. In the 1890s Châtillon-Plessis became the editor-in-chief; he also wrote the book *La Vie à Table à la Fin du XIXème Siècle*, an anecdotal history of the world of cuisine during the fin-de-siècle period.

L'Art Culinaire was the community bulletin board for elite French chefs during the heyday of their organizing efforts for the profession as a whole. Here they elucidated their theories on cuisine, promoted their professionalizing projects, exchanged recipe and menu ideas, explored the cuisine of other nations, and, of course, pontificated on the need to keep French haute cuisine on top of the culinary pyramid. In the Christmas issue of 1888, Achille Ozanne, resident chef-poet of the journal, published a long piece, "L'Art Culinaire," that tells in eloquent verse the master narratives of the journal: the ceaseless struggle of the budding cook to attain skill and mastery and the ongoing battle of France to maintain its national glory.

> C'est en vain qu'en cuisine, un simple rôtisseur
> Pense d'un grand talent être le possesseur:
> S'il ne sen point, chez lui, la passion ardente
> Qui de ses premiers pas s'est faite confidente,
> Il tourne dans un cercle où son esprit captif,
> Aux choses du progrès semble toujours retif.
>
> —O vous, qui de notre Art, embrassez la carrière,
> Sachez sacrifier presque la vie entière,
> Afin devenir cuisinier de talent:
> Le début est aride, et le succès est lent.

> It is in vain that with cuisine, a simple grill-cook
> Can think that he possesses a great talent:
> If he doesn't have within him, an ardent passion
> That with his very first steps, they are done with confidence
> He will turn in a circle with his spirit held captive
> And matters of progress always out of reach.
> O you, who know our Art, embrace the career,
> Know that you must sacrifice almost your entire life;
> To become a talented cook:
> The start is barren, and success is slow.

Four stanzas later he continues:

Le grand siècle apparut, où toutes les sciences
Brillèrent par l'éclat de leurs magnificences
Sous Louis XIV, on vit aux soins du Grand Vatel
Du Prince de Condé, fameux maître d'Hôtel
La Cuisine brillante et déjà reputée
Comme Art dont la valeur n'était pas contestée.
Et toujours poursuivant la route du Progrès
L'Art culinaire alors devint un Art français
Déjà les Cuisiniers étaient des personnages
Dont les réels talents se soldaient à bons gages
Quand parut Beauvilliers qui fut le Créateur
Du cuisinier pour tous, nommé restaurateur.

The great century appeared, where all the sciences
Shone by the light of their magnificence.
Under Louis XIV, we see the great Vatel under
the patronage of the Prince du Condé, that famous nobleman,
The brilliant cuisine already renowned
As an art whose valor was not contested
And always in pursuit of the road to Progress.
The culinary art thus became a French art.
Already cooks were characters
Whose real talents paid off with security
When Beauvilliers appeared, who was
The creator of cooks for the public, and named restaurateur.

As seen in this poem, the literary, artistic, and gastronomic components of the journal were generally used in the service of the professionalizing aims of the chef-writers. These men (especially in the early days,
1883–93) were single-minded in their goals. In 1886 Henri Second, a
journalist who reported on the Parisian culinary world, wrote in "Cuisine
et Cuisiniers" for the periodical *France* that *L'Art Culinaire* was started
while members of the Société des Cuisiniers Français were waiting for
their professional school to be founded. During the first ten years of
"the school on paper," as the editors called it, the vast majority of articles
concerned plans for this (they hoped) state-sponsored culinary school
and the culinary expositions that were mounted to raise money for this
much discussed and much desired new institution.

The Exposition et Concours Culinaires, a major vehicle for the Société des Cuisiniers Français, was started in 1882 to raise money for the

culinary school, but after the school's demise it became a means to promote French culinary trades more generally. Display—visual, commercial, technical—was the major preoccupation of these expositions. The long hall was dominated by huge center tables full of complex set-pieces, both savory and sweet. The edges of the hall had booths where commercial vendors displayed their wares. And somewhere, kitchens had to be set up so that young apprentices, master chefs, and housewives could perform for the culinary competitions The sites for the expositions changed from year to year; in 1888 in the Pavillon de la Ville de Paris and another year in the Salle Wagram. The Société was always eager to get official sanction for the expositions because by association sanction would also be provided for the school. For the culinary expositions they had the official patronage of the minister of commerce and industry and the Conseil Municipal of Paris.

The Société des Cuisiniers Français was the chief organizer, but it often teamed up with other associations in the food trade; for example, in the 1888 exposition the Culinary Societies of France and the Alimentary Societies and Unions were involved.[17] That year the exposition was held February 18–25; the price of admission was three francs on the first day and one franc on subsequent days. The cooking demonstrations and competitions were held only on the first day, probably the reason for the higher price. All profits were to go to the Ecole Professionnelle de Cuisine.

L'Art Culinaire published numerous articles on the expositions over the years. Since the Société des Cuisiniers Français was the chief organizer of the events, the journal provided information about where and when an event was being held and how people might participate. They also published articles that reviewed and critiqued the expositions. An article reviewing the 1886 exposition talks of the "grand, the immense, the gorgeous success" of the exposition, with more than twelve thousand in attendance. According to the editors, the exposition was a success because "for 48 hours the public spirit was preoccupied with the many efforts of a *corporation* which is most often neglected and not given the merit it deserves." They quote the Préfet de la Seine, who was given a full tour of the exposition and then gave comments to the public, voicing his support of a cooking school to train aspiring young chefs, for "as cooks [*cuisiniers*], the whole world depends on you, because French chefs are spread everywhere."[18]

Just as French chefs were a transnational phenomenon in this period, so were the culinary expositions. In 1885, two years after the first culinary expositions in Paris, a similar exposition was held in Willis's Rooms in

London. The London exposition was the brainchild of Edouard Pouard, a French chef employed in London. In the initial years of the British expositions, the main intent was to introduce British consumers and cooks to French haute cuisine. Most of the entrants were French chefs living in Britain, and the food prepared for display and competition was French haute cuisine. The members of the jury who awarded medals were almost exclusively French—in 1887 Jules Gouffé and Alfred Suzanne were on the jury. Members of the public who came to see the displays included the French consul, Baron Rothschild, and General MacDonald.[19]

The displays in London were almost identical to those in Paris; maintaining a unified front of French haute cuisine was of great importance to the chefs organizing the British exhibition. For example, one dish exhibited in London was a boar's head on a pedestal elaborately decorated with a hunting motif. The boar's head, rimmed with several cooked quail, was speared with the ubiquitous garnish of the day, six *hâtelets*, or skewers garnished with decorations like crayfish and artichoke hearts.[20]

In the end, the journal survived longer than the much anticipated, discussed, and heralded Ecole Professionnelle de Cuisine. After 1894, when it became clear the professional school was going to close because of lack of sufficient enrollment, the journal became less focused on meeting specific professional goals—the culinary school and the culinary expositions—and promoted larger concerns of the culinary community. In 1896 the cover advertised that its contents included discussions of "Cuisine moderne universelle," "Hygiène et Sciences Naturelles," "Services des Hôtels et Restaurants," and "Pratique Professionnelle." These articles indicate a desire on the part of French chef-organizers to incorporate contemporary trends and values about food into their more specific aims. The journal also advertised that its staff included representatives from all countries and reporters from all the cities of the globe.

The international reach of French chefs continued during the 1890s and into the early 1900s, despite the fact that chefs from France were still unable to learn their art in a professional school and continued to be trained via apprenticeships in the workplace. In France their social position was precarious, but in the world beyond their "Frenchness" continued to make them desirable and elite laborers. New York City's hotels, clubs, and restaurants served French haute cuisine, prepared primarily by chefs hailing from France. Delmonico's, where the kitchen was run by Charles Ranhofer, served French delicacies such as game pâté, allouettes in aspic, and timbales of foie gras. Perhaps reflecting the fact that the profession of chefs was more socially successful outside than inside

France, the later issues of *L'Art Culinaire* provide numerous articles on the activities of French chefs in locales such as America and Italy and information on the cuisines of other cultures.

The Cook as Ouvrier: Le Progrès des Cuisiniers and *Chambres Syndicales*

Not all people involved in professional cooking during the second half of the nineteenth century were chefs de cuisine. At the pinnacle of the professional kitchen hierarchy, the chefs de cuisine ruled over a vast number of other workers—sous-chefs, garde-mangers, cuisiniers, aides de cuisine, pâtissiers, and so on. Though their professionalizing aims via the Société des Cuisiniers Français and *L'Art Culinaire* included the interests of people in the lower echelons of the kitchen, especially the adequate training of all workers in the kitchen, there were other issues of work—improvement of working conditions, fair hiring practices, guaranteed wages, to name a few—that they did not address. Other associations and journals founded in the same period addressed such concerns, and these can be seen as "trade" associations and journals.

The first such trade journal was *L'Etoile* and the first trade association was the Société des Secours Mutuels des Cuisiniers et Pâtissiers-Glaciers, which was founded in 1868. Conflicting reports exist on what laborers were considered eligible to be members and the relationship of the Société to the journal. It is reported that the journal was initially started with "garçons des restaurants" in mind. Perhaps laborers in "public" kitchens were the earliest targeted audience, and as they became more organized the journal shifted to being the official organ of the Société des Secours Mutuels.[21] The earliest of the professional culinary journals, it was published weekly with a circulation of 1,200 to 2,500, and only lasted one year, apparently because of suppression of the press by the French state. A prevailing concern of the journal was the creation of a viable replacement for the guild system, especially for that system's ability to protect workers and take care of their own in times of distress—illness and old age. The Société des Secours Mutuels would incorporate the role of a workers' aid society, and membership, among other things, guaranteed that "once the Secretary admits a worker into his new family, if he ever falls sick, once he informs the managing director, the director will send him the appropriate medicines as soon as possible."[22]

The other goal of the journal echoes that of *L'Art Culinaire*: the adequate training of young boys into the world of work. In an open letter to all his colleagues on the front page of *L'Etoile* on April 5, 1874, the managing director laments: "I must say that among our young men there has been very little progress in the art of cuisine." He attributes the problem to ineffective apprenticeships: "Je vois beaucoup d'hommes et malheureusement peu d'ouvriers" (I see plenty of men, but unfortunately few workers).

Though *L'Etoile* and *L'Art Culinaire* were allied in their commitment to the promotion and maintenance of high standards in culinary practice, in *L'Etoile* this commitment has a more political tone. This is partly because of the larger scope of occupations involved in the associated Société, but it is primarily because the editor, Charles Virmaître, explicitly pursued the connections between workers in the food trades and the French working class. Of particular interest to him was the growing desire to transform the largely apolitical mutual aid societies into the newly evolving and more political active organization, the chambres syndicales (trade union chambers).

Virmaître's agenda for people in the food trades reflects larger changes in occupational organization between 1860 and 1890. After the passage of the 1864 law on the right to coalition, strikes became an increasingly common feature of French life, and the chambres syndicales movement became more powerful and organized. At the Universal Exhibition of 1867, workers' delegations petitioned the minister of commerce to sanction chambres syndicales, and this petition was accepted. The combination of successful organization and state sanction gave great impetus to workers' movements; the most dramatic consequence of the increasing politicization of workers was the Paris Commune of 1870.[23] The chambres syndicales were among the few organizations not suppressed after the failure of the Paris Commune. By 1884 a law, defended by Waldeck-Rousseau, was passed that gave all organized chambres syndicales legal rights. The trade unions were still under state jurisdiction, however: they were bound by law to provide their statutes and membership rolls to local police authorities.

The history of the organization of chambres syndicales for the food trades during the 1870s and 1880s parallels the trajectory of trade movements for other labor practices in France. After an initial burst of energy and interest around the time of the Commune, when two thousand cuisiniers were members of some chambre syndicale, the movement went into a decline, and from 1878 to 1883 there was very little activity.[24] The state sanction of trade unions in 1884 helped precipitate their revitalization. In early 1885 the more narrowly defined Chambre Syndicale pour Cuisiniers de Paris was started, and by 1887, at the First Workers' Congress of the Cuisiniers of France, held in Paris from March 29 through

April 2, this organization decided to initiate a nationwide "Fédération Générale des Cuisiniers Français." Ultimately the federation included the local unions of Bordeaux, Lyon, Algiers, Marseille, and Toulouse.[25]

Thus, though Virmaître himself was unable to organize culinary workers with his journalistic writings in the 1870s, by 1884 his desire for the development of a chambre syndicale for the food trades was fulfilled. At that same time, *Le Progrès Gastronomique* was started to provide information for cuisiniers, pâtissiers, confiseurs, and glaciers; it was published under the auspices of the Chambre Syndicale des Cuisiniers-Pâtissiers de Paris. This version of a chambre syndicale and an accompanying journal lasted for only a year because it was decided that the different skills of workers encouraged smaller organizational groupings. The primary aim of the chambres syndicales in the early days was to facilitate relations between workers and patrons, especially in regard to hiring practices.[26] Interestingly, the first editorial of this journal states its aims in much more generalized terms than *L'Etoile* (seemingly its predecessor), and in fact the language is much more reminiscent of *L'Art Culinaire*. Because the latter journal was started just a year earlier (in 1883), perhaps the discourse of the culinary community had become more unified in the seven years since *L'Etoile* had folded. The first issue begins with the following:

NOTRE PROGRAMME
To maintain French Cuisine and Pâtisserie at the rank they have been assigned over the centuries, that is the aim to be followed by the Chambre Syndicale des Pâtissiers-Cuisiniers in publishing this professional journal.

To provide our students with those indispensable elements and right principles which will later allow them to become artists in the culinary art, these are the considerations which have guided the members of this association in the founding of *Le Progrès Gastronomique*.[27]

Thus, even though the chambres syndicales engaged in organizing activities similar to other trade unions of the time to obtain support for their concerns, if this announcement is any true indicator, the more narrow concern of the maintenance and promotion of their expertise and knowledge in French cuisine was just as important.[28]

In accord with these aims to maintain standards, the journal contains many "recettes professionnelles," for one way to assure the consistent quality of culinary production was to have people producing similar dishes. One recipe is for canard à la Rouennaise, a fairly simple dish compared to some other "haute" preparations. The reader is instructed to flambé the duck, carefully truss it, and then return it to the pan and brown it in butter. The next instruction is to put the duck in a casserole with carrots, onions, thyme, parsley, bay leaf, and a little wine, and finally, after the duck is roasted, to finish the liquid with espagnole sauce. Such a recipe, classic in configuration but fairly simple to execute, would have functioned as an excellent standard-bearer for cooks in all ranks of the professional hierarchy.

By 1885 the cuisiniers and pâtissiers had broken up into two separate chambres syndicales, and a new journal was founded for the more specialized Chambre Syndicale des Cuisiniers: *Le Progrès des Cuisiniers*. The journal's slogan was "Un Pour Tous, Tous Pour Un" (All for One and One for All), a battle cry that indicates the existence of a unified culinary community.

The story of the founding of the chambres syndicales and their early struggles to gain acceptance within the world of working chefs and cooks confirms the growing sensibility that a culinary community existed in Paris, even if its members' specific social and political aims were not always identical. A number of cuisiniers decided to form a chambre syndicale solely for cuisiniers because they believed that a union was the only effective way to have their particular occupational concerns understood by state and society. During the first eighteen months of its existence, there was very little support for the organization because existing organizations initially saw the Chambre Syndicale des Cuisiniers de Paris "not as an ally, but as an enemy,"[29] ready to invade already marked ground. Eventually, however, the association was accepted into the "bosom" of the Union Universelle pour le Progrès de l'Art Culinaire because it was fully accepted by the most powerful organization of the era—the Société des Cuisiniers Français. This association, in the words of associates at the chambres syndicales, had "gathered together cuisiniers of all orders, notably those [employed in] the principal bourgeois houses and restaurants of Paris" and "had created amicable relations with cuisiniers who work abroad with culinary contests and exhibitions." It understood the necessary but somewhat different tasks of the Chambre Syndicale des Cuisiniers.[30]

The daunting task of the chambre syndicale was the "general emancipation of all cuisiniers," a phrase that highlights the major political differences between the two associations. The chambre syndicale was interested in attaining state sanctions to help improve the day-to-day working conditions of all men working in professional kitchens. In this regard the organization had several principal thrusts. The first goal to improve the physical conditions of the kitchen, primarily to insist on proper light and ventilation because public kitchens were often located in the basement. Another was to lobby the Conseil Municipal and the Chambre des Députés to revoke a law allowing for private job placement bureaus because these bureaus had a reputation for taking advantage of unsuspecting workers. A third goal was to attain membership in the Conseil de Prud'hommes, and a fourth to lobby the state to pass a law requiring one day off a month for all cuisiniers.

Thus the chief goals of the association journal *Le Progrès des Cuisiniers* were the promotion of these political agendas and, as for *L'Art Culinaire* and *Le Progrès Gastronomique*, the continued maintenance of consistent culinary standards and the promotion of the complexity of their expertise in order to attain higher occupational status.

"In all truth, who are we really in today's society? Some say *artists*, some simply state *workers*. Of those two appellations, which is the truth?"[31] wrote Philéas Gilbert in a stirring article in *Le Progrès des Cuisiniers*. Gilbert explores the contradictions embedded in the characterization and categorization of labor practices in French society at the time, and implies that indeterminacy at the larger level of French state and society fuels the insecure position of the culinary community. "We are one and the other, but we cannot easily be one and the other. If you look closely, we are really not one or the other." This frustrating situation is externally derived. "Are we ouvriers? Yes! Are we considered as such by the law? No! Are we artists in all senses of the word? Yes! Are we given the social consideration due to all artists? No! Thus we are neither workers or artists. Who are we? Nothing! What do we want to be? One and the other!" He concludes in a fairly despairing tone: "How can it be that a science for which men have dedicated their whole lives does not have a higher place on the social ladder?" Appropriate categorization by French society, in any legitimizing form, seems to elude these men.

Occasionally, dissension broke out between the two main culinary organizations. These conflicts concerned which organization could claim credit for activities such as the culinary expositions, and thus they were more turf wars than ideological battles. In 1891, by which time both organizations were fully established in the Parisian culinary world, some members of the Chambre Syndicale des Cuisiniers de Paris protested the high-handed attitude of the Société des Cuisiniers Français in assuming it could make all final decisions about the culinary expositions. Members of the Société responded that their organization had truly invented the expositions, and this gave them right to more control?[32] To the outsider, turmoil of this sort indicates the success of the expositions for both groups because they both wanted to lay claim to them.

Schools: The Unifying Theme

The Société des Cuisiniers Français and the Chambre Syndicale des Cuisiniers were consistently in agreement on one fundamental point: the best means to power—social, political, or economic—was through knowledge. In that sense there was a unified consciousness among culinary laborers that their most important priority was to promote French haute cuisine as the unique property of male workers in the public sphere. They knew that their best chance at claiming a protected market for themselves as professionals, artists, or workers lay in their claim to an esoteric and difficult body of knowledge that would be their ticket to occupational stability and ultimately, elevation.

As early as 1874, in *L'Etoile*, Virmaître was discussing the need for a culinary school in France. In one article he discusses the shameful fact that a school to train young boys to be cooks had already been started in Britain, but nothing had been done in France; he points out that, ironically, one of the reasons for founding the English school was to loosen the French stranglehold on the public kitchen by training British boys in proper cooking technique.[33]

The discussion of the importance of starting a school continued through the 1880s in all the professionally oriented journals: *L'Art Culinaire*, *L'Etoile*, *Le Progrès Gastronomique*, and *Le Progrès des Cuisiniers*. It took almost twenty years from the time Virmaître made his plea until the Ecole Professionnelle de Cuisine was founded, primarily because the men involved in organizing the school considered official approval and financial support of the French state pivotal to the long-term success of the school. The difficulty in attaining this support helps explain the endless promotion of the unique glory of France's cuisine by all the men involved in haute cuisine at that time. They needed to convince those at home as much as abroad of the importance and complexity of their labor. In the end, the school was financed primarily with the money raised by the Société des Cuisiniers Français in their culinary expositions and through private donations. The Paris gas company also donated a large gas and coal oven.[34] In a letter to the Minister of Commerce, Monsieur Berenger, president of the Société, addressed the relationship of the French state to the school:

We know that the State, which has so many worries, does not always have the means and we don't have the intention of asking for more than it can give. What can be given by the State for our work is less financial than moral support. That is an effective and affirming gesture, a sign of strong patronage which elevates and honors our efforts and encourages our work.[35]

Other schools for the manual trades were fully supported financially by the state, but for various reasons the French government decided that a cooking school was not a high financial priority.

The official title of the school was Ecole Professionnelle de Cuisine et des Sciences Alimentaires. It was "created under the auspices of the Société des Cuisiniers Français and under the patronage of the Minister of Commerce, Public Powers, and the Culinary Associations and Employers of Paris and Abroad." Patronage here simply meant a governmental stamp of approval. Thus in the end the only way the Ecole Professionnelle could be started was with private funds, and it had to settle simply for state patronage.

The regulations of the school, published in *L'Art Culinaire*, reveal that the men of the Société des Cuisiniers Français had a complex and ambitious vision for the school. The regulations state that the primary aim is to "educate and train practitioners in all the branches of the culinary arts and the nutritional sciences: Cuisine, Pastry, Confectionery, Liquor, Wine, Cooked Meats, and Conserves."[36] The outlined course of instruction has three components. The first, an Elementary Course, includes a preparatory section, a study of the elementary principles of pastry and cuisine, domestic economy and hygiene, and gas cookery. History, geography and botany, from the "point of view of cuisine," are also included in the curriculum. At the end of this course there is an exam, and a Certificate of Culinary Studies is awarded. The second course, a Superior Course, develops more intensively the skills and knowledge promoted in the Elementary Course. Animal anatomy, meat and fish carving, decoration of dishes, and the culinary applications of molds and models are all required classes. At the end of this course, if the student successfully passes a set of exams, Professional Diplomas will be awarded. Finally, there is a Preparatory and Elementary Course open to the public, for young girls and housewives. The rules state: "These classes and courses are intended to spread the taste for well-prepared meals, and to teach the principles of hygiene and domestic economy." If the female students attended regularly and passed an exam, they received a Certificate of Elementary Studies.

Figure 7. The first professional culinary school in Paris. Harvard College Library.

There were two requirements for enrollment as a student at the school: to be between the ages of fourteen and twenty and to be a French citizen. Both requirements arose from the professionalizing concerns of the founders: allowing foreign or trained boys into the school would undermine their ultimate aims of creating an exclusive market for professional French chefs. (An exception was made for auditors, who could be of foreign extraction if the governing council made a special case). The cost of the Elementary Course was twenty francs a year; for the Superior Course it was fifty. Scholarships were available and would be granted after due deliberation by a council made up of representatives of the school, the state, the city of Paris, and professional culinary associations.

The physical plan of the school included a classroom for "courses in theory and practice," a model kitchen, a dining room, and a wine cellar. Other plans included a reading room and library that would be open to students, personnel of the school, and members of the Société des Cuisiniers Français, as well as a Museum of Culinary Arts.

Despite the fact that the school had a well-conceived curriculum, a location on the Rue Bonaparte near the Ecole des Beaux-Arts, a complete administrative structure that included a supervisory council comprised of nine members of the Société des Cuisiniers Français plus three other members for the larger culinary community, a school director, and an endowment, it did not last more than two years.

The Ecole Professionnelle did not fail to become a part of the training process for men in the culinary world because it ran out of money: on the day of the dissolution of the school three thousand francs remained in the bank. Men involved in the founding of the school, such as Châtillon-Plessis, hint darkly about "discontented internal elements" who wanted to sabotage the aims of the school.[37] More plausibly, Philéas Gilbert says that a major problem was lack of commitment on the part of the students, which arose from two major constraining factors. The older, already accepted method of learning via hands-on apprenticeship did not disappear with the founding of the school, and many restaurant and hotel owners were ambivalent about the school, because if this newer model of training took precedence over the traditional apprenticeship system, the owners would lose a tremendous opportunity for unpaid labor in their establishments.

Professional Rule

The ideal-type of professions—medicine and law—which concern so much academic literature, emerged from the fluid and cacophonous nineteenth-century world of occupations. Because of the chasm between the real and the ideal, origins and outcomes should be understood as distinct in a discussion of the professionalizing process. As we have seen in the organizing efforts of the Société des Cuisiniers Français, and the Chambre Syndicale des Cuisiniers, institutionalized higher education was understood as vital to both the professional and trade models for the organization of production developing in the late 1800s. But translating an ideal model to a real system of higher education and truly attained high status for their occupation proved more difficult than these men imagined.

Magali Sarfatti Larson's distinction between the word "profession" and a concept of profession comes to mind when we try to place the practice of cooking as a labor form in modern capitalist society. Though she acknowledges the use of the term "profession" more broadly, Larson argues that " 'profession' is thus a name we give to historically specific forms that establish *structural links between relatively high levels of formal education and relatively desirable positions and/or rewards in the social division of labour.*"[38]

It would be a mistake to deny the importance of these men because they did not succeed in making the practice of cooking into a proper "profession" as it is defined sociologically. The story of the French chefs does not end with the closing of the Ecole Professionnelle on the Rue Bonaparte in 1893. The historical acts involved with the development of the profession during the late 1800s—the establishment of schools, associations, expositions, and journals, acts which were reactions to changing class structures—had the ability to determine the fate of cooking practice. Though deprived of state-sanctioned institutional power within their own country, the chef-organizers continued to dominate in the supranational domain of hotel, restaurant, and club kitchens. Their continued international presence and organizational efforts after 1893 did provide them with a long-term reputation for being the masters of "hauteness."

Despite the supposed failure of cooking practice to become a profession in the strictest sense of the term, the practice did not lose its elite aura. To this day, few question the rule of France in nondomestic cooking practice. How is French haute cuisine's ongoing rule as the canon for expert culinary knowledge justified today? An answer often given by people inside and outside France, professionals and amateurs, comes from the perspective of sensory evaluation: French cuisine dominates because in an absolute sense it is better. A slightly more complex view, but one that also derives rationale from the sensory domain, is provided by the French and is put most succinctly by the public relations director of Centre Ferrandi, the premier Parisian school for education in the food trades. In response to the question, "Why is French cuisine considered great all over the world?" she stated, "Mais c'est simple. Ici nous avons le goût" (But that's easy. Here, we have "taste"). An administrator and teacher at the Cordon Bleu school in London suggested that the climate and geography of France facilitated a varied agricultural base and that the greater array of raw ingredients enabled France to have a more complex cuisine than Britain. All these arguments for French haute cuisine's hegemony come down to the view that French dominance is the result of a set of attitudes and practices that are unique to the French people and the French soil.

Other explanations can be generated, however. I would argue that beyond a sensibility with cultural nationalist origins, the dominance of French haute cuisine in the public sphere can be seen as a case of imperialism, especially if we define imperialism as "the practice, the theory, and the attitudes of a dominating metropolitan center ruling a distant territory."[39] Usually imperialism is understood in association with colonialism; the former as the ideology of domination and the latter as the concrete mechanisms of control and power. Obviously, French culinary imperialism has obviously never had the depth or breadth of effect (especially in regard to extraction of natural and human resources) of, for example, British colonial rule in India. But if the domination of particular forms of knowledge is considered an important, even vital part of the enterprise of empire, then the history of France's rule in the culinary domain serves as an instructive case study.[40] In the gap between the professionalizing aims of the chef-organizers and the less than perfect outcomes of their efforts, much can be learned about the myriad complexities of the division of labor under capitalism and the long-term power of workers' associations and journals in the modern period.

7 CULINARY EXPOSITIONS IN BRITAIN AND FRANCE

The Englishman makes an excellent administrator, and if he could only combine his administrative ability with the Frenchman's genius for cooking he would make a first-rate chef. But this will not be the case until his training is improved. The art of cooking must be studied and followed regularly as a profession, not adopted by hazard, as is often the case with English cooks. When we have reformed and improved the present apprenticeship of the cook in this country, and have learned to regard cooking as no longer a menial occupation, but a distinct and honourable art or profession, which must, like any other calling, be properly learned and studied, we shall in course of time have a body of English chefs who may be able to hold their own in competition with foreign artists.[1]

Though the status of their occupation was a major preoccupation of the chef-authors writing in professional culinary journals such as *L'Etoile*, *Le Progrès des Cuisiniers*, and *L'Art Culinaire*, other topics are discussed. One is "l'art de la cuisine." Sometimes the complexity and artistry of a certain dish are analyzed. More often, however, these are works of advocacy; the authors espouse the merits of their practice and argue that their terrines, pièces montées, and galantines should be considered works of art. Their desire to define a standard of cooking and to maintain that cooking is an art comes as no surprise given their professionalizing aims. However, as has been noted, French chefs had a difficult time convincing the larger society that their practice should be rewarded with the status of profession because the boundaries to their expert knowledge were so difficult to maintain. Neither education nor gender nor place could contain cooking as an expert practice. Cooking had trouble being considered anything more than domestic drudgery, let alone a discipline capable of producing art.

There is another reason for the chefs' difficulties: the emergence of a widening gap between the definition of *craft* and *art* in larger European society in the period of their most intense professionalizing activities.[2] The emergence of an abstract definition of "art" to categorize certain activities only became part of general usage in the second half of the nineteenth century. Before that time the term "art" or "artistry" had been used to refer to a type of skill or skillfulness.[3] Scholars interested in other craft forms have documented the developing demarcation between labor that produces craft and labor that generates art with the demise of the guild system and the rise of industrialized forms of production.[4]

As Deborah Silverman has noted, after the Revolution in France there emerged a distinction between the artist and the artisan: the beaux-arts included painting, sculpture, and architecture; the decorative arts everything else.[5] Because the French had a long-standing reputation for the quality of their cultural productions, the French state became increasingly invested in their protection. Initially more concerned about the beaux-arts tradition, by the late 1800s the French government became more involved and supportive of crafts and craftsmen. Notably influential in this transition from state dismissal to state support were the growing crafts movements outside France, Britain and Belgium being the most influential. The French state became increasingly concerned about international competition in arenas of craft production traditionally dominated by the French.

Among the people involved in these practices, concerns often revolved around the place of the various artists and artisans in the social order. One concern was the treatment of the artist or artisan in society. Another, perhaps more of a social critique, revolved around whether the beaux-arts were in fact a tool used by emergent bourgeois societies to align themselves with the highest echelons of elite culture, the aristocracy.[6]

The Belgians and British involved in the arts and crafts movement envisioned their activities as part of an attempt to restructure their societies. The French, generally speaking, were much more concerned with "aiming to elevate artisans to artists in the existing academic institution[s]."[7] Domestic objects, such as tables and rugs, no matter how highly elaborated, were not considered fine arts. Silverman sees the French approach toward the growing shift between artists and artisans as clearly nondemocratic. Rather than seeking to democratize art and give it to the people, French art nouveau sought to aristocratize the crafts, to extend the hierarchy of the arts to include the artisan.[8] The French chefs writing in journals like *L'Art Culinaire* and forming organizations and schools adopted much the same approach.

During this period, function frequently demarcates the contrast between "art" and "craft." With function as the dividing factor, as long as their "professional cuisine" remained connected to food and nourishment, for all the valiant efforts of the French chefs, the fight to have their cuisine considered an art was invariably going to be an uphill battle. Once the chefs were outside France, however, the battle for artistic recognition and superior status was easier to win.

The emergence of a craft-art divide is roughly historically parallel in the Britain and France, but certain skilled forms of labor, although the works had a clear function, escaped being neatly categorized. Architecture is an example of a productive practice hovering between craft and art that in Britain was seen to have a Continental history, which gave it a superior status. The French discourse and practice of architecture (particularly the model for training derived from the Ecole des Beaux-Arts in Paris) helped architectural practice in England to be perceived as much art as craft in popular discourse.[9]

Culinary Expositions

A vehicle for promoting the artistry involved in the production of French haute cuisine was the culinary exposition, the first of which was organized by the Société des Cuisiniers Français and took place in 1883. These expositions were an excellent method of showing the French (and soon the British, American, and German) public, through visual displays of a whole array of sweet and savory dishes, the capacity for food to be transformed into objects of artifice. Such amazing feats of transformation—from a set of raw ingredients emerges a towering three-dimensional edifice (a castle made of sugar paste, a whole decorated fish on a pastry boat)—could only impress on the viewing public the skill and expertise of those involved in their production.

Expositions, or in the Anglicized usage exhibitions, were extremely popular during the nineteenth century as arenas where products could be displayed. Initially, these events were organized primarily to promote international trade, most specifically to sell the products of national industry and craft. France was the first country to develop a national policy that supported the exhibiting of wares for the purposes of promotion, but Britain was soon to follow. In fact, it was fear of British encroachment on traditionally powerful French craft industries that helped impel the French to stage such national expositions (another instance of the complex cross-Channel rivalry as to who best owned and produced elite culture). Throughout the early 1800s, expositions were based on the promotion and display of products seen as the results of nationalist undertakings, and therefore, though expositions were taking place throughout Europe, only products of the host nation were on display. It was not until 1851 that the "Great Exhibition of all Nations" was held in London, the first of the many world expositions that became such an important part of the dissemination of ideas about culture, nation, and civilization by the turn of the century.[10]

Explicitly national expositions were still held, however. Throughout the 1880s, the period when culinary expositions were initiated, French officials were fearful that France's reputation as the seat of sophistication was on the wane. They wanted to keep attention focused on France; the Paris Exposition of 1889 was a product of that concern. Silverman remarks on this nationalist preoccupation by the French state: "Official reports were no longer marked by absolute confidence that France would keep its monopoly of 'le bon goût' and 'l'originalité.' America, the country without a history, and Germany, the leviathan of blood and iron, particularly alarmed French officials by demonstrated unanticipated agility in creating useful objects tastefully and elegantly embellished."[11] The culinary expositions of the period 1880 to 1910 were direct descendants of the national exposition.

The culinary expositions were organized to promote a cultural production certainly capable of "le bon goût": French haute cuisine. Though they might consider themselves fortunate if their creations were considered even a craft, the organizers hoped that the elaborate set pieces on display and the culinary competitions would show the viewing public that cooking was indeed an art. Culinary expositions, launched initially in Paris, were held in London by 1885. The theme was the same: show people the artistry of French haute cuisine. This was possible in Britain because so many French chefs were working there at the time, and the British public embraced the "high" status of the cuisine.

Over the years, and in all the locales where they were held, these events were extremely consistent in their conceptual and physical construction. The focal point of every event consisted of the long tables that ran through the middle of the exhibition halls, so that viewers could see all sides of the exhibits. Sometimes a table would be contain only one complicated, multi-dish spectacle created by members of a culinary association, or a culinary school, or a hotel kitchen. More often, one long table would include a variety of dishes created by individual participants.

Figure 8. Culinary exposition in Tours, 1892. Harvard College Library.

A photograph of the 1892 Culinary Exposition in Tours shows a hall
set up in a manner that suggests both a decorative arts exhibit and a
dining room where an extremely ornate banquet is about to be held. The
table on the far left looks ready for a dinner party: napkins are neatly
folded and placed on top of plates that ring the perimeter, and flowers
and branches make an elegant border around the display dishes rising
from the center of the table. The dinner party displays were often produced by the kitchen of a well-known Parisian restaurant; at a 1913 exposition, Henri-Paul Pellaprat, under the auspices of La Varenne St.
Hilaire, had a table with seven different dishes, including gailles glacées à
la Carmen and ananas à l'Impérator.[12] The more complex single set-
pieces can be seen on the two longer tables to the right.

The more commercial component of the event is relegated to the
edges of the hall. The perimeters of the exposition are lined with exhibit
booths where vendors display individual products for sale. The exact
names of the product cannot be read in this picture, but a review of a
later exhibition in London provides detailed descriptions of the trade
exhibitors. The vendors were from all over Europe, and many of the
displays were of a single product produced in a factory; the company
making Bovril, the Shredded Wheat Company, and the Swiss Macaroni
Manufacturing Company were all represented. Other vendors showed

Figure 9. Culinary exposition in Paris, 1892. Harvard College Library.

Figure 10. The awards certificate from the 1891 culinary exposition in Paris. Harvard College Library.

"the highest class of comestibles," like Messieurs Goslin and Company of London, who made fancy prepared foods: "Among the dishes which deserve special mention were the boned pheasants and ballotin of larks, chaudfroid de cailles, and galantine of chicken; also a damier de foie gras, dressed boar's head, dressed tongue, and delicious-looking pressed beef."[13] These purveyors of prepared foods had already provided an initial transformation of food into an object of artifice worthy of haute cuisine.

Overall, the participants in the culinary expositions were broken down into two broad productive categories: artistic and trade. Cuisine, pâtisserie (pastry), and confiserie (candy) made up the artistic group; the trade group consisted of alimentation commerciale, boulangerie (bread), boucherie (meats), charcuterie (pâtés, terrines, sausages), poissonerie (fish), légumes (vegetables), and so on.[14] The message in the photograph concerning the place of food and food production in modern French society has two aspects. The pyramids of canned goods with their company logos emblazoned on signs above leave little doubt as to the commercial importance of the exposition, especially for marketing certain products and individual skills to the consumer/viewer. The aesthetic impact (on all the senses) would have been just as powerful, however.

The tables in the center of the hall are dramatic enough, but when they are combined with the curtain swags, chandeliers, candelabras, and floral displays the room becomes nothing short of spectacular.

The aesthetic impact on the viewer can be imagined by looking at photographs of set pieces from a culinary exposition in New York. These three dishes, "A Mighty Hard Road," saumon à la Neptune, and pâté de gibier Impérial, are each paradigmatic examples of the most complex manifestations of the three-dimensional dish of which proponents of French haute cuisine were so fond. "A Mighty Hard Road: A Raines Law Idea" is a case of "dish as narrative"; it presents a visual picture of an ongoing political debate in the state of New York over the legality of hotels serving alcohol on Sundays, an unfortunate loophole in a law otherwise written to combat prostitution and lewd behavior. A policeman is depicted carting away a wagon of "hayseed legislators." Subjugating food to politics in such a literal sense was a fairly unusual occurrence, and this dish was probably only produced for that exposition. No recipe for it has been found, and one wonders if it was actually an edible edifice. The ingredients for the construction of the piece are not clear from the photograph; perhaps it was made from sugar paste, perhaps pastry. The conflation of food and political commentary in this dish shows the wide spectrum along which those involved with these culinary events chose to interpret what was possible in the creation of culinary artifice.

Saumon à la Neptune is much more typical of the sorts of dishes on display at culinary expositions between 1880 and 1910. Especially familiar is the placing of the main dish on some type of pedestal, itself covered in decorations made from food. This form of presentation could be found in Carême's day. These socles were often made out of lard and flour and sometimes rice that was cooked, puréed, and pressed into molds. Here the part of the dish guaranteed to be edible, and potentially even tasty, is the whole poached fish in the center.

Pâté de gibier Impérial is also representative of the usual three-dimensional productions often found outside the exposition, at large hotels and private banquets. In this case, raw ingredients have already been transformed into a cooked food of a consistency that can be shaped in an artistic fashion. Here, game pâté has been molded into a three-tiered cakelike shape and decorated with real flowers. The edifice has been placed on a pedestal that looks like a tree trunk; perhaps this more natural setting reminds the viewer that this is a savory and not a sweet creation, like the wedding cake it very much resembles.

In the medieval period, the complex displays, the stuffed swans and marzipan trees dangling with fruit, revealed the status of the consumer, particularly the host of the grand feast. By the turn of the twentieth century, this aspect of haute cuisine said as much about the producer. These set pieces took an incredible amount of time to create. Complexity in presentation and involvement of time were required elements in the production of displays categorized as "artistic" at all the expositions: in fact, complexity and involvement equaled artistry in the developing ethos of the culinary profession in this period.

Perhaps these were standards that could be judged at the level of skill, the domain those involved in a practice hovering in the gray area between art and craft could best control. The challenge of going far beyond the function of the dish, to enter the world of sign and symbol, separated the artists from the nourishers. The drawing and recipe for saumon à la Humbert Ier, a silver medal piece from the 1885 Exposition and Concours Culinaire in Paris, reveals how symbolic a dish can become and the diligence required to get to that point.

Recipe for Saumon à la Humbert Ier

Choose an attractive male salmon that weighs approximately 5 kilos.

Scale and gut the fish. Wash it well, and wipe it dry. Replace the stomach with a farce [mousse] of a smaller fish; stitch up the stomach and wrap the fish completely in a large piece of office [brown] paper coated with oil. Place it on a fish grill so that stomach touches the bottom of the grill. Put the grill in the fish poacher.

In the fish poacher place four bottles of white wine from Capri, a quart of tarragon vinegar, thyme, bay leaf, peppermint, onions, carrots, and salt [in proportion]. Put in enough water to completely cover the fish. Place it over a high heat, when it is about to boil, put it on the back burner of the stove, and let it boil very slowly for 15 minutes.

At this point this is a fairly straightforward recipe for poached fish, though the addition of a fish farce inside the original salmon could tax the average bourgeois housewife or her domestic servant. What happens next, however, goes beyond any functional definition of a fish dish. The salmon is transformed into a political symbol.

Remove the fish poacher from the stove and let the fish chill in its own juice. After it has cooled completely, carefully remove the grill, and leave it to drain for three hours, or until it is very dry. Remove the paper, and let it dry for another hour. Take a white fish demi-

SAUMON A LA HUMBERT Ier

Par M. Giovanni Canali

Concours Culinaire de Paris (1885) — Médaille d'argent

Figure 11. Saumon à la Humbert Ier, silver medal winner from the 1885 culinary competition. Amy B. Trubek.

glace and with a brush lightly cover the fish, so it has a clear and shiny "cover." Put it carefully on a plate where you have placed a pedestal made of rice. Cover the fish with a stronger glace than the first; than, make a very strong mayonnaise for garnish, and with a cornet [small piping tube], imitate the design on the drawing. Take four hâtelets [skewers] and garnish with cooked crayfish; insert them on an incline into the back of the fish. Then take a kohlrabi and trace onto it the crown of Italy; imitate the diadem [jewels] with sweet peppers and carrots, and in the middle place gilded leaves. Sprinkle the crown with brilliantine and place the crown on the head of the salmon. The eyes can be made to look natural with mayonnaise, and the center of the eye can be made with cooked egg white. In the mouth of the fish put a camellia made out of a beet.

By this point the fish is no longer so much a fish as it is a testament to political power, a gesture of international unity on the part of chefs, here Giovanni Gavali, a French-trained chef of Italian origin. Here we see how nationalism has in fact become a type of artistry. The fish may be named for the Italian ruler, but the decorations on the platter, while ostensibly glorifying Italy, really promote the French nation:

The four small baskets on either edge of the platter are made by hand out of radishes; in each you place two small roses made out of carrots and fried parsley.

The four custards found on each side of the fish, decorated in the three colors of the Italian flag, they should be made with a fish-based gelatin and a macedoine of vegetables spread through all three layers. You should make the gelatin in three parts: the first white, the second colored red with red peppers from Spain, and the third colored green with spinach. Decorate 4 molds on the bottom with egg white cut to look like the "star of Italy" and for the other 4 imitate the petals of Margarite.

Cover slowly with gelatin and a hash of pistachios, and then put some more gelatin on top. After that, put some diced green beans into the mold and than some green-colored gelatin. Finally, put the small flowers made of brussels sprouts which you cover with white-colored gelatin. Finish it off with a macedoine of vegetables covered with red gelatin. Unmold on the plate. Cover the rest of the plate with chopped clear gelatin and fried parsley. Serve with a mayonnaise and a ravigote sauce.[15]

Despite the celebration of Italian nationalism in the design, this recipe is highly characteristic of French haute cuisine. Each dish is in fact a compilation of an entire series of smaller preparations joined together to create an ensemble whose impact on the viewer will be similar to seeing a three-dimensional sculpture. The linkages between the smaller parts (the molds, the baskets, the fish) are primarily visual; commonalities or even resonances in terms of taste are secondary. Thus the primary function of the molds created to evoke the Italian flag is to reinforce the regal theme of the dish: the recipe for preparing the molds contains no mention of seasoning, for example, even the most basic salt and pepper.

Critics of French haute cuisine complain that this method of cooking does not let the flavor of ingredients stand on their own. Elizabeth David remarks disdainfully about haute cuisine being "pompeuses bagatelles de la cuisine masquée."[16] Her comments, which appear in an English cookbook called *French Country Cooking*, are intentionally in French, criticizing the elitist attitudes of French chefs. According to such critics, the concern of chefs with making their practice "artistic" creates an haute cuisine with perhaps more visual impact than taste, a critique strikingly similar to the one levied at medieval haute cuisine by contemporary scholars and cooks. But an elaborate, colorful three-dimensional sculpture can be more easily perceived as art by people attending expositions than even the most delicious coq au vin championed by David in her cookbook—a stew of a vaguely brown color. After exploring the incredible symbolic and structural load brought to bear on this one set of culinary techniques and principles, it comes as no surprise that quality of the flavor was subjugated to intricacy of the display.

Culinary expositions chiefly promoted culinary expertise by creating spectacular visual experiences for the consuming public, but for those involved in making these amazing concoctions they were also competitions: prizes were awarded to the "best" in various categories. For the organizers of the expositions, who were also the organizers of the Ecole Professionnelle de Cuisine, holding competitions was another means of delineating the standards for mastery considered so essential to the success of the profession. Medals were given out at the Paris events by the minister of commerce; as at the Olympics, the medals were gold, silver, and bronze.

One of the competitive categories was for apprentices. At the 1887 exposition, an apprentice named Seng, working at the maison Chiboust, was awarded a silver medal for his entry: a horn of plenty (also known as a cornucopia) made of nougat and garnished with glacéed fruits. The reviewer compliments the apprentice's creation and says that for a young man he is extremely knowledgeable in sugar work. The reviewer compliments another prizewinner for his lobster in aspic, especially for the excellent application of a unusually clear aspic.[17] Note that these evaluations do not concern themselves at all with the taste and flavor of the dish, but rather focus on the excellence of presentation.

The critical emphasis on mastery of execution according to primarily visual criteria is also seen in a positive review in *L'Art Culinaire* of a piece at the 1885 London Exposition by Monsieur Mallet. The display piece is a temple; the frame is made of wood and all the decorations of royal icing. "As a whole, the piece is gracious, the proportions are good, the spire is bold, the design of the grill which surrounds the base of the monument is magnificent and the execution of the entire piece is done with great lightness and consistency; we see the hand of a conscientious and capable artist."[18]

The reviewer thinks the piece should have won an award; the reasons it did not reveal the fine line between edibility and artistry in the displays at culinary expositions. "The jury did not give the same encouragement to Monsieur Mallet by awarding him a certificate of merit . . . because the frame is made of wood." The reviewer feels this is not a just critique: "what if Monsieur Mallet, the creator of this beautiful monument, had made a frame with thick layers of royal icing . . . and on top of that done his decorating work, would anyone have scratched to look and find the truth?" The decision by the jury to question M. Mallet's craftsmanship because of his use of a wood frame spurs the reviewer to pose a series of difficult questions. "Where does the work exist? Is it in the frames? The presentation boards have no real use. The beauty of the work is in all the small designs, the small ornaments, etc., etc., and the correct proportions of the piece as a whole, and Monsieur Mallet has accomplished those things with distinction."[19] The fundamental concern lies in the appropriate definition of aesthetic sensibility and aesthetic evaluation when food is the art. The judges of the displays decided that edibility, or more accurately, the use of raw materials understood to be edible, and therefore food, was necessary for any piece of work to be awarded a prize at their event, which was, after all, a culinary exposition.

The London Culinary Expositions

The first culinary exposition in London was held in 1885 at Willis's Rooms and was chiefly organized by Edouard Pouard, a French chef working as the caterer to Queen Victoria's Body Guard at St. James's Palace. Pouard borrowed directly from the Parisian exposition, from the physical layout of the room, dominated by the long tables covered with white tablecloths, to the type of food: "The first exhibition, in 1885, as already stated, was organized with the object of making a display of essentially French Cookery."[20] It was also advertised as "an exhibition of High-Class Cookery."[21] Thus, as in Paris, the displays at the London event consisted chiefly of complex three-dimensional set pieces. A photograph of a medal-winning table at the 1893 London exposition shows at the center a massive dish, essentially a three-foot-high pyramid made entirely of whole lobsters and crayfish resting in rows, all heads pointed toward the pinnacle, where a statue of Venus is perched.[22]

The genealogy of the London exposition reveals the influence of the Parisian chef-organizers. As mentioned above, Pouard, a member of the Société des Cuisiniers Français, went to the Paris exposition and decided to organize a similar event in London. He did that under the auspices of the Culinary Society, a small organization of fewer than twenty men, all French.[23] By 1889, after four successful expositions, more people working in food trades in London wanted to be involved, and a new organization, the Universal Cookery and Food Association, was founded. The primary initial aim of this association was to organize the London expositions, but it eventually became a very important part of the organization of the cookery profession as a whole, and went from 186 members in 1892 to 1,325 in 1906.[24] A genuine offspring of the Société des Cuisiniers Français, the Universal Food and Cookery Association played a very similar organizing role to its Parisian parent: its members organized expositions, published a journal, and were involved in the promotion of schools for teaching young boys.

The food on display was very much the same, but there were other differences between the expositions held in London and Paris. Essentially, the differences were related to variations in the explanatory categories for the food on display and the range of people involved in producing the food. The categories for the culinary competition were more class-based in London than in France, perhaps reflecting the more rigid class structure in place in Britain by that epoch. The categories were household, artisan, and high-class or artistic cookery. The types of dishes produced in these categories varied in their nation of origin; household dishes retained an English touch but high-class dishes came directly from the haute culinary tradition. Household and artisan exhibits concerned economy and nutrition as much as skill. English cuisine was emphatically not part of the culinary knowledge necessary for success, and thus the linkages between high-class, artistic cookery and French haute cuisine were more clearly drawn.

Women were more involved in the London expositions as well. In Paris, the majority of exposition visitors were women, and some women who attended Auguste Colombié's and Charles Driessens's cooking classes were involved in culinary competitions. There is no evidence, however, that women taught any cooking classes in Paris or were members of professional associations.[25] In London, on the other hand, women were involved in teaching and running cooking schools and in the organization of the expositions. The work of the female students of Agnes B. Marshall, who ran the Mortimer Street School of Cookery in London, filled an entire section of the hall at the 1885 exposition (and the display won a silver medal). Marshall was also a member of the jury that decided on the prizewinners.[26] In a country that was not their own, the French chefs apparently did not perceive this involvement of women, so closely linked to the domestic sphere, as threatening to control over culinary expertise.

Women, Art, and Artifice

There is no denying that an immense amount of skill and creativity went into the production of the complex pieces on display at the culinary expositions. It is not sufficient, however, to begin and end the analysis of these events, so important to members of the culinary community in this period, with a discussion of specific pieces. The relationship of these concoctions to the larger world of cooking and cuisine at that time must also be considered.

A great distance lay between the grandiosity of the displays and the commonness of the cooking performed by most of the people attending the expositions, that is, women cooking in the domestic sphere. In these halls the complex and often contradictory relation of professional and domestic cuisine was frequently under debate. Lucy Yates notes this problem in her review of the seventeenth Universal Cookery and Food Exhibition in London in 1906. She spent a day walking around the exhibition halls, through the large crowds, and came away with the following sense of what people thought:

> The severest censure was given to some of the elaborate efforts of the professional artist, and judgement, less severe, but not less frank, was passed upon the failures of the humble housewife and cook to reach the supposedly correct standard. The serious young cook, whose mistress had paid for her admission in the hope that she would return primed with new ideas, looked overawed by a sense of the unattainable, while the French apprentice seemed disposed to be disrespectful to the work of his superiors. Mature housewives, accustomed to a daily wrestling with the problem of "What shall we have for dinner?" looked rather disappointed, and were heard to pronounce sentence somewhat after this fashion:—
>
> "If you ask me, I say things ought to look just what they are, and not be made to imitate something else. All this glazing and sauce-making and fiddle-faddling can only be done by people who have nothing better to do. I wanted to find a new pudding for Sunday's dinner, and can't; if I'd wanted to lay out a ball-supper, it would have been a different matter."[27]

This is not an accidental response. Women played a vital role in these events by their attendance and participation in certain competitions (if they were associated with cooking schools). But for the organizers the culinary expositions were explicitly designed to impress, even intimidate. The chefs of the day aimed to promote a set of skills that were expressly far distant from the practical concerns of domestic cookery.

Women's attendance was important for the expositions, but they were not members of the culinary club (and if Lucy Yates is an example they were not concerned about membership). Auguste Escoffier's thoughts on male versus female culinary skills were presented in a speech he gave on a visit to the United States and excerpted in an American culinary journal. His elision of male professional chef with the production of art is clear, and has much to do with keeping distance between the public and domestic spheres, between skilled labor and everyday work. Also relevant is the fact that Escoffier's words were reprinted in a professional culinary journal in the United States: the task of maintaining separate and unequal abilities in cooking was an international one. He begins by making the claim that cooking is an art:

> Cooking is undoubtedly a fine art, and an accomplished chef is as much of an artist in his particular branch of work as a painter or a sculptor. There is as much difference between good cooking and bad as between a symphony performed by a great master on a first-rate instrument and a so-called melody played by some out-of-tune barrel organ.

He quickly goes on to qualify that claim; only some are capable of making cooking into an art.

> In the ordinary domestic duties it is very hard to find a man equalling, much less excelling, a woman, it is her sphere in life; but cooking rises far above a mere domestic duty; it is, as I have said before, a fine art. The reason that in cooking the palm has always been awarded to "mere man" is not far to seek. It is not because man is more epicurean than woman, for this, though maintained by women, is not a fact. Woman is quite as fastidious over her food as man,—as the ordinary man—and bestows as much thought on her meal as he does. It is simply that man is more thorough in his work, and thoroughness is at the root of all good, as of everything else. A man is more particular over the various little details which are necessary to make up a really perfect dish. . . . None are too important for his consideration.
>
> A woman, on the other hand, will manage with what she has handy. This is very nice and obliging of her, no doubt, but it eventually spoils her cooking, and the dish is not a success. One of the chief faults in a woman is her want of accuracy over the smaller items—the exact amount of flavoring, the right condiments to each dish; and that is one of the chief reasons why her cooking pales before that of a man, who makes his dishes preferable on all occasions to hers.

Escoffier ends with a call to the artistic intentions of the male chef, the dedication and focus he puts on the proper execution of each and every dish:

> To a chef his work is a joy forever, and he invents new dishes with as much pride and care as a modiste or a milliner creates some new gown or hat; and he carefully studies the trifling details of each separate flavor before he sends his new masterpiece of culinary art before his patrons. When women have learned that no trifle is too small for their consideration, then we may find them at the head of the kitchens of the chief clubs and hotels; but until then there will certainly be at least one place where man can reign supreme.[28]

There is what Escoffier parades, but also what he betrays.[29] He shared the opinion of the predominant figures in the culinary community of the day that women could be cooks, but they could not be expert cooks, artists. Artistry was a gendered category for chefs involved in producing French haute cuisine. They knew the importance of women to the status of their practice, but at the same time they believed it was important to make a clear distinction between cooking performed by males and cooking prepared by females.

Written in the 1890s, Escoffier's words come from a France concerned with a new type of female: the *femme nouvelle*. Journals of the time probed the consequences of the "new woman" in France. There was ongoing concern that too many women, now educated, were beginning to have professional aspirations.[30] However, as a result of the shifts in the social division of labor occurring in France at the time and the apparent demise of craft occupation, male chefs were as concerned as the new woman with the possibility of attaining professional stature. Hence Escoffier's male/female, professional/domestic, making-art/making-do division of culinary labor. The desire to be a professional, an artist, was part of a larger inclination to not be other things and to avoid any suggestion that the practice of chefs had links to activities lower in the social division of labor. The practice of chefs was cooking, so they were particularly concerned with disengaging themselves from the association of cooking with women's work, work that occurred solely in the domestic sphere. Thus the desire to separate the work of the professional chef from the work of the housewife was partly a result of the traditionally gendered connotation of cooking. They needed to construct their expertise so that, in very clear terms, the larger society would see that their practice was completely separate from the domestic sphere. This could effectively allow them to have professional power, if defined as the control over exclusive knowledge in terms of both content and access.[31] "You'd best stay home and cook in *that* kitchen" was the chef's message to the bourgeois housewife empowered by new ideologies of identity and looking to find her area of expertise.

Though male chefs and female cooks often protested the actions of the other, some allegiance across gender lines occurred. The female visitors to the culinary expositions in Britain and France were to some degree allied by their class, and the judges of the entries were allied by their commitment to a shared set of standards and skills. The cooks and chefs were unified in their desire to display mastery and finesse over the elaborate cuisine of the day. And all those involved agreed to the power of French haute cuisine.

EPILOGUE

No single causal factor explains the power of France in the public sphere, why, in particular, French haute cuisine came to define the practice of the modern culinary profession and the discourse on fine food. The culinary techniques and the aesthetics of presentation used today are derived from principles, methods, and standards developed in France. The symbolic significance of French haute cuisine cannot be denied, eventually extending to include place, people, and practice. Genealogical investigations thus lead back to France, but ultimately place becomes more symbol (of elite culture, of mastery) than simple earth, rock, and water.

From the beginning, haute cuisine was in demand only among elite members of European society. Only after 1800, with the rise of the bourgeois public sphere during the nineteenth century, did the "high" part of French cuisine come to have a broader social impact. A new class of bourgeois consumers emerged who paid attention to French haute cuisine; their consumption was both literal and symbolic.

A well-organized, highly nationalist group of French chefs also appeared. Clearly the actions of French chefs helped solidify a new cuisine—professional cuisine—which was born of a new social, economic, and political milieu. The ethnographer's investigation of French chefs reveals the vital and interconnected role of institutions, journals, cookbooks, skills, symbols, and values in the historical maintenance of French haute cuisine.

Professional cuisine emerged from France in this period, but it was ultimately not contained by either the time or the place. Cuisines are usually associated with particular territories, however, and the most widely used geographic parameters are national. The discourse on cuisine is a nationalist discourse: we talk and write about French cuisine, Thai cuisine, Roman cuisine. Anthropologists certainly do when they examine the methods, values, and rules that structure a cuisine. This seemingly logical connection between nation and cuisine, however, fails to incorporate other social and environmental realities that also shape the content and character of a cuisine. With a concentration on the nineteenth-century community of chefs and bourgeois, fissures appear and the traditional reliance on the "nation" to analyze cuisine seems limited. This is especially true in a case study of these professional chefs because their vocation was transnational in nature and international in reach. In fact, they helped create a completely new cuisine that was shaped by the market, consumed by members of the public, and above all, made by people committed to the complexity and superiority of this culinary knowledge.

Almost a century after the tireless efforts of French chefs such as Gouffé, Dubois, Ozanne, and Escoffier, what is the status of the professional cuisine they worked so hard to create and promote? Status remains a preoccupation, though there have been important tectonic shifts and new strata have appeared, especially in the type of food served and societal perceptions of the professional cook or chef. To this day, expertise in the profession continues to be based on achieving mastery of a set of techniques and methods derived from classic French haute cuisine, although the system of mastery is no longer as rigidly defined. The past twenty years have witnessed some changes in professional culinary practice, particularly the increased presence of other national cuisines—Italian, Japanese, and Thai—on fine dining menus. Many argue, however, that these influences are primarily at the level of flavor rather than in the areas of technique and method. For example, the chef-owner of an Italian bistro in London who trained in France believes that the fundamental procedures he uses in preparing his bistro fare are all French in origin and that the Italian-ness of his bistro comes from the use of certain ingredients (olive oil over butter) and certain dishes (pizza or pasta). He said he prefers to hire French-trained chefs because they know "all the basics."[1] It appears that at this point in time, France as nation or elite culture means less to this chef than France as the source of the methods and techniques of professional cooking.

The complete dominance of French haute cuisine and French chefs in restaurants, hotels, and clubs has certainly ended; food influenced by other cuisines is being made more and more by chefs who hail from the United States, Britain, Italy, Thailand—in fact, from all over the globe. Women are now accepted in professional kitchens, even if at times grudgingly. Many contemporary chefs in the United States cook food that is an amalgam of French culinary technique and exotic ingredients; the influence of Asian cuisines is particularly strong now. (Fillet of sole with a citrus-coriander beurre blanc and braised shortribs with a tamarind sauce come to mind.)

The power of the French haute cuisine remains, however, in consumer choice and culinary training, sometimes to the chagrin of the new, more multiculturally directed American chefs. One chef I interviewed owns two highly successful restaurants and was in the process of opening a third. His restaurants are known for their spectacular interiors, and his food is a complex marriage of American Southwestern and Mexican flavors and technique with French aesthetics of presentation. He happens to have also pursued graduate studies in anthropology at a major state university before he left to become trained as a chef.

As a noted chef who is interested in the cuisine of the Americas, Mark Miller is concerned about what he calls "the Eurocentric bias" in American restaurant culture and in American culinary culture more generally. He thinks that with food, as with all parts of the aesthetic realm, there is a "mental picture that controls perception," and traditionally in America this aesthetic gaze has been turned toward France. The training of chefs in American culinary schools is one locale where he sees such a bias being perpetuated. As he puts it:

At [a leading culinary school], French food in its technique and recipes is seen as superior: dominant is the given and superior is the assumption. For example, when students make a curry, they spend three days making the veal stock, and then they pull the box of curry powder off the shelf. They don't make curry powder from scratch, they don't have a curry chart where they can change any one of the twenty ingredients; they don't understand the differences between North and South and Muslim and Hindu. They don't understand the multitude of expressions curry can have. So we have a reinforcement again that whatever is French is important, and whatever is not French is not important.

They [the students] have a Eurocentric palate. But we don't have a Eurocentric world anymore. [There is] an unconscious re-affirmation of the Eurocentric model. Not only in its techniques, tastes, and culture, not only [do you produce] the re-affirmation of these, but you also [produce], in effect, a hierarchy that puts ethnic food below. The acceptance of ethnic people and ethnic culture is below the European one as well. A culinary caste system is being set up, and it is being reaffirmed all the way along: symbolically, linguistically, technically, and taste wise."[2]

Later in the interview, Miller made a very telling remark about the economic impact of the Eurocentric bias in American culture. He said that, although his restaurants are extremely popular—they are always full and people book reservations weeks in advance—he can never charge as much per entree as a less renowned French restaurant in the same city. In his view, the reason for this glass ceiling is directly related to American social values, particularly the traditional high value put on European cultural productions. Whether or not the dishes are executed properly, especially in the realm of flavor, a French restaurant can always charge higher prices purely because of a general assumption that the meal's "Frenchness" permits it to be expensive.

Producers and consumers still sustain the French legacy in the public sphere. Culinary producers, the people blithely pouring six-month-old curry powder purchased in sixty-ounce containers from S. S. Pierce into the pot in the course of making their lamb curry, have been trained to focus on stock and not on curry powder. The culture and cuisine caste system that impedes Miller creatively and financially is being produced and reproduced in the same social institutions where it was first invented: hotels, clubs, and restaurants. Much to his chagrin, Miller sees the power of France both in the training of culinary professionals and in the spending decisions of wealthy and middle-class consumers. When Americans want a fine, expensive meal, French haute cuisine still beckons.

Spectacle and complexity continue to define professional culinary practice and fulfill consumer desires to assert elite status. Such efforts now literally realize such expectations; "height on the plate" is the latest trend in the haute style of presentation. Small molds such as timbales are used to layer vegetables into a stunning display of color (layers of eggplant, tomato, and carrot, for example) and are unmolded directly onto the dinner plate. Desserts have become sculptures: chocolate boxes, gilded candies, and ice cream molded into pyramids with a chocolate banner at the top are all normal preparations.

The attitude of consumers toward professional chefs in contemporary society has been profoundly altered in the past decade, however, at least in the United States. In a culture that worships celebrity, champions individual achievement, and cherishes personal time, the chef has become a figure of merit. Twenty-five years ago, people knew the names of great restaurants in New York, Boston, or San Francisco, but they rarely knew anything about those who cooked the food. Now Americans eating in elite restaurants are so curious about the practice of cooking fine food and those who do it that there are windows that look into kitchens, kitchens set up in the dining area, and special tables available so customers can eat dinner in the kitchen. In the United States, the rising status of culinary professionals and consumer interest in their practice roughly parallels the dramatic rise of women joining the workforce. As women take flight from the domestic sphere, perhaps cooking is becoming esoteric knowledge. Finally, cooks and chefs can create the closure around their expertise necessary in order to become a "profession."

Chefs host cooking shows on television, write celebrity cookbooks touting "their" cuisine, hire publicists, and are profiled in *People* magazine They are featured in advertisements. As in the nineteenth century, however, these are merely the most elite cadres of kitchen workers. Most cooks still labor in anonymity for low wages in hot kitchens. The average starting wage for a line cook in a high-end restaurant is approximately eight dollars an hour. Work weeks often run to fifty or sixty hours, and cooks still stand on their feet all day, lift heavy objects, and work in cramped surroundings. The reputation of the successful chefs has drawn more and more people to culinary schools, hoping to capture some of the glory; dozens of new culinary programs have opened up in the past decade.

As Robert Darnton says, "The questions keep changing and history never stops."[3] The past twenty years have brought shifts in France's own culinary values and practices. Recent magazine and newspaper articles have dramatically heralded changes in consumer preferences; their titles include "Sushi Cordon Bleu? Foreign Food Invade[s] the Land of Haute Cuisine" and "The Precious Few: French Haute Cuisine Is Hanging in There—Barely."[4] These articles discuss two behavioral shifts among the French. First, many young French citizens want to explore new, exotic flavors when they go out to eat and thus are rejecting the traditional bistro for their restaurant meals. They want to consume le Tex-Mex, le cheeseburger, and le sushi. Second, the costs of running a grand restaurant serving haute cuisine are becoming exorbitant, which makes the average cost of a meal at an establishment serving haute cuisine outside the reach of the French bourgeoisie. Some older chefs such as Joel Rubochon are closing their temples of hauteness, and other chefs are opening "baby bistros" or branches that serve fine food cheaper and faster. In response, Patrick Martin, vice president of Le Cordon Bleu, says: "If France is to maintain respect for its culture, it must open to other cultures. We're teaching our students to apply the techniques of French cooking to international products and tastes."[5] To Rubochon, who closed his three-star Michelin restaurant in 1997, this signals the end of France's rule in the realm of the haute: "Cuisine has become banal. All around the world we eat the same things, whether we are in New York, Tokyo, Rome, London, Paris."[6]

Many culinary historians, chefs, and gourmets from outside France have pointed to the quantity and quality of specialized food historically available in France as a sign of its culinary superiority. There has always been a depth to the cuisine because of the many fine artisans involved in preparing all types of food for the public. Comparing Britain to France, the instructors at Le Cordon Bleu often bemoaned the dearth of good bakeries and butchers in London, the preponderance of industrially prepared food, and the rise of large supermarkets. Contemporary American chefs who have lived in France, Alice Waters for example, point to the ready availability of excellent ingredients—cheeses, vegetables, breads, sausages—as a reason for France's culinary greatness. She has tried to recreate the French style of food distribution and preparation in America. Throughout her professional career in northern California, Waters has developed and supported a network of small purveyors who provide food for her restaurant, Chez Panisse.

The past twenty years have witnessed a tremendous increase in the availability of high-quality ingredients locally produced. A French chef who has cooked in New York for forty years noted that when he first arrived he had many of his ingredients flown in from France. He now gets almost all his products from nearby farms in Long Island, Connecticut, and New Jersey. Another executive French chef of an elite French restaurant in New York has purchased his own farm on Long Island and grows food for the restaurant. Many American chefs now identify their culinary style with their use of local, fresh ingredients and their dedication to seasonal dishes.

At the same time, French haute cuisine has begun to recede as the defining influence during training at culinary schools. At the New England Culinary Institute students are no longer given Saulnier's *Répertoire de la Cuisine* when they register. Two new classes have been added in response to the more global reach of fine dining menus: Taste and Flavor and World Flavors. At the Culinary Institute of America, a class called Asian Cuisine acknowledges that students are as likely to be interested in the complexities of different types of soy sauce as different methods for making stock. Young American chefs now often join two new professional associations: the Chefs Collaborative and the International Association of Women Chefs and Restaurateurs. The charter of the Chefs Collaborative extols chefs to use only the freshest locally grown ingredients and makes no mention of France or French cuisine. Women have become major figures in the culinary profession, a fact that illustrates the changes in society that have occurred over the past fifty years.

The commonly held assumption "if it is French, it must be fancy" has a complex genealogy stretching back into modern European history where culture, status, consumption habits, and culinary practices emerge entangled with meanings that outlast their time and place of birth. A complex set of social realities (concerning class and culture), social values (concerning taste and art), and social practices are implicated in the construction of this (apparent) cultural truism. An analysis of French haute cuisine's dominance in the public sphere therefore addresses larger intellectual queries concerning definitions of culture, processes of class formation, aesthetic values, and hierarchies of taste. As Priscilla Clark has stated, "Cuisine is not food, it is food transcended, nature transformed into a social product, an aesthetic artifact, a linguistic creation, a cultural tradition."[7]

These issues raise a series of questions. Are the only standards to judge whether cooking is an art those created by French chefs in the nineteenth century? Should we broaden our horizons and say all cooking done by a trained professional is a form of art? But given the enormous breadth and depth of cooking practice, does that mean that the criteria of standards, mastery, and tastefulness so important to the nineteenth-century European definition of the culinary arts would be forfeited? Or can we devise a theory of culinary "art" that transcends time and place and judges creations—whether sole à la meunière, shrimp in black bean sauce, or roast lamb with mint jelly—on a culturally and historically objective plane? But then, would everyone making them be a chef? They certainly would all be cooks.

This book is part of a larger inquiry that seeks to understand cuisine beyond the nation and develop new frameworks for understanding this profound element of our material life that is fundamental to survival and vital to the economy, but also important to our sense of sociality, pleasure, and well-being. Since the nineteenth century professional chefs have transformed the nature of food as it is prepared and the perception of food as it is consumed. Despite cultural shifts and economic transformations, they are still the masters of hauteness.

One legacy of the French culinary empire is the continuing use of French terms to describe techniques and dishes, despite the fact that in many professional kitchens no native Frenchman can be found. In fact, many aspiring chefs take a class in culinary French in culinary school. The importance of French terms and the ensuing confusion for many non-French speakers, have been present ever since the French began publishing cookbooks and cooking for people outside France. The December 1907 issue of the English culinary journal *The Epicure* discusses this problem: "Our plain food, even when good and well served, is often lacking in those little additional touches which give it variety and make it appetising. We tacitly acknowledge this when we seek, on occasion, to present it *à la mode Française.* . . . Let me now try to unveil a few of those secrets of variety, giving at the same time the correct definition." It then goes on to define eighteen French sauce names, including these:

A la Jardinière means a collection of cooked vegetables used daintily as a garnish, or in combination with meat in stews, or as cut small and freely introduced into soups.

A la Macédoine means also a collection of vegetables cut small, but set in white sauce, and generally is confined to green vegetables garnished with others. It also means a collection of fruits embedded in jelly.

A l'Espagnole means not a typically Spanish dish, but one of a dark savoury nature in which brown Espagnole sauce figures.

There are always secrets to unveil about French haute cuisine. At the same time, in contemporary professional kitchens, the definitions of techniques and dishes may be known, but they are often contested. Chefs can vehemently disagree about the best way to julienne a carrot, make a béchamel, or create a fumet. What follows is a brief list of French culinary terms mentioned in the book, but among culinary experts there may be some disagreement. This glossary should be considered suggestive, not definitive.

ASPIC: the intensely flavored jelly made from heavily reduced clarified stock. Can refer to a way of arranging cold dishes where slices of chicken, game, fish, vegetables, fruit, and so on are set into molded jelly (or gelatin).

BALLOTTINE: a small galantine of fowl or poultry leg, stuffed and poached in an appropriate broth.

BÉCHAMEL: a savory white sauce made with white roux, milk, and seasonings.

BRUNOISE: vegetables cut into perfect half-inch cubes.

CHARLOTTE: a molded dessert made with custard and ladyfingers.

CHAUDFROID: this term can refer to meat dishes in savory aspics served cold, but also to the sauce itself, often a béchamel with added gelatin.

CONSOMMÉ: stock that has been concentrated and clarified of impurities.

CRÈME À L'ANGLAISE: a cooked dessert custard made with egg yolks, sugar, and milk.

EMULSION: a homogeneous mixture combining two repulsed liquids; examples in cooking are vinaigrette and mayonnaise.

FARCE: at the broadest it means to stuff, but it traditionally refers to a meat or vegetable filling that often includes bread crumbs and is used to stuff meat or fish.

FONDS DE CUISINE: fundamental stocks, or the pan drippings from cooking meat that are used to flavor a sauce.

FUMET: a fish stock.

GALANTINE: a whole fowl or poultry, boned and stuffed with a fine forcemeat, often shaped to resemble its original appearance and poached in broth.

GRANITÉ: a crystallized, not churned, sorbet-type iced dessert, often made with fruit and sometimes with wine or liquor.

JULIENNE: very thinly sliced vegetables, usually one- to one-and-a-half inches long and one-eighth of an inch thick.

LIAISON: a type of thickening designed to give body to sauces; typically eggs and cream or animal blood.

MIREPOIX: A mixture of carrots, celery, and onion, finely diced and added to sauces to improve flavor.

PÂTÉ: Usually made with ground meats, fish, or offal, often encased in a savory pastry crust.

ROUX: equal parts flour and fat cooked over a slow heat. The type of roux depends on the cooking time and the color of the final product. Definitive thickening agent of the cuisine.

TAMIS: a flat, drum-shaped, fine mesh sieve.

TOQUE: the tall, starched white hat a chef de cuisine wears at all times. The height of the hat worn in the kitchen traditionally denotes the status of the cook or chef.

CLASSIC RECIPES OF FRENCH

HAUTE CUISINE

What follows is a selection of recipes for dishes mentioned in the book, representative of French haute cuisine and published between 1870 and 1910. They have not been tested to see if they would work in a modern home kitchen, rather they are presented to show in greater detail the shape of a recipe and a dish in this period, when French haute cuisine in the public sphere was in greatest demand.

Socle

A pedestal made out of edible ingredients, a socle raises a dish to provide a better view. They are an important part of the aesthetics of French haute cuisine, and the decline of the socle with the greater use of the service à la russe is of concern to many chefs. As Jules Gouffé notes in *Le Livre de Cuisine*, pp. 597–98, the elaborate decorations of the cuisine provide an elegant scene for the consumer, and show commitment to the craft on the part of the cooks.

In an article from *La Cuisine Pratique*, Charles Durand instructs the reader how to make Mousseline de Jambon à la Royale. He breaks the lesson down into four parts: 1) Learn how to make a socle or pedestal out of rice; 2) Learn how to make a white chaufroix [sic]; 3) Line and decorate the inside of a mold; and 4) Decorate the finished Mousseline de Jambon à la Royale. Below is a translation of the recipes and instructions for making the socle. By the late 1800s, you do see some cookbooks move to the fairly formal and scientific style of recipe presentation we are accustomed to, with the ingredients separated from the technique and method section. Since the text is really a written-up version of a live demonstration these are presented in a narrative.

To present a decorative plate such as this, it is necessary to make a pedestal, either out of stéarine or rice.

I will prepare the pedestal in the latter fashion, which needs to be done several hours in advance so it can chill completely. To this effect I put in a casserole a kilo of rice, which I have carefully washed ahead of time in cold water. After having covered the rice in cold water, I place the casserole on the flame and then I have stirred it with a wooden spoon until it has just begun to boil.

After boiling for six minutes, I take the rice off the heat and let it cook until it has just absorbed all the water and it can easily be crushed with pressure from the fingers.

I then put the rice in a mortar where I finely grind it and next pass it through a tamis, all while it is still hot, so that it becomes a firm paste which I line the inside of a mold which has been liberally buttered.

Meanwhile, with the remaining rice paste I make a croûton of the same height and width as the middle of the mold which will be used to place the bread for the ham mousse. When the rice paste in the mold is completely chilled, I dunk it for a minute in warm water and unmold the rice which will be the pedestal for the final piece.

Fillets of Sole Véronique

This recipe comes from the English language version of Auguste Escoffier's *Le Guide Culinaire*. This sole dish became very popular in fine dining restaurants and hotels throughout Europe and the United States and can still be found on menus today. Escoffier's book was also written in a narrative style, probably because he aimed it to a professional audience and thus assumed the reader had some familiarity with technique and method.

Lift out the fillets of sole; beat them slightly; fold and season them, and put them in a special earthenware, buttered dish.

With the bones, some of the trimmings of the fish, a little minced onion, some parsley stalks, a few drops of lemon juice, and white wine and water, prepare two spoonfuls of *fumet*.

This done, strain it over the fillets, and *poach* them gently.

Drain them carefully; reduce the *fumet* to the consistency of syrup, and finish it with one and one-half oz. of butter. Arrange the fillets in an oval on the dish where they have been *poached*; cover them with the buttered *fumet*, and set to glaze quickly. When about to serve, set a pyramid of skinned and very cold Muscatel grapes in the middle of the dish.

Put a cover on the dish, and serve immediately.

In his glossary of terms, Escoffier defines poaching as follows: "This term means cooking very slowly in small amounts of water at the lowest temperature." He describes fumet as "a kind of concentrated essence extracted from fish, game, by slow cooking."

Consommé au Tortue or Potage de Tortue Verte au Claire

Turtle soup was considered an extremely sophisticated dish. Numerous recipes for this soup can be found in cookbooks and magazines of the period; two are included here. One is from the English culinary journal *Food and Cookery* of April 1904, initially excerpted from Adolphe Meyer's book *The Post-Graduate Cookery Book*; the other is from *The Epicurean*, by Charles Ranhofer's (the chef at Delmonico's restaurant in New York for decades). Both recipes were aimed at professional chefs, so they make a large quantity.

POTAGE DE TORTUE VERTE AU CLAIRE

The best and most profitable turtles are those weighing from 100 to 150 pounds. When ready to be decapitated, lay the turtle on its back, cut off its head with a sharp strong knife, stand it head downward in a tub and make an incision between the hind fins and the upper shell, thus allowing the blood to escape more freely. If time permits, let the turtle lie in a cool place over-night.

The following morning place the turtle on its back on a table, and with a sharp knife cut out the under shell, gradually removing all the meat which is attached to it; then cut off the fins and separate them from the fleshy parts to which they are attached. Detach the intestines and throw them away.

Divide the shells in four or more pieces, plunge them (as well as the fins and the head) into boiling water (for a few moments only, but long enough to enable you to remove the horny outer skin), and then lay in cold water.

For a turtle of 100 pounds, have ready the following stock (which can be prepared the previous day):

Stock: Put into a stock boiler 25 lbs. of shin of beef and 25 lbs. of knuckle of veal; fill with 15 gallons of water and set on the fire. When boiling, remove the scum and add 4 fowls partially roasted; garnish with 5 carrots, 2 turnips, 3 onions, 6 leeks, and 2 stalks of celery tied together, and add also a good handful of salt; free the stock from scum and fat occasionally and let simmer for 4 hours; then strain the broth and put aside for further use.

Place the cleaned turtle shells and fins in a large stock boiler, moisten with the stock prepared as above, and place on the fire. When boiling, remove the scum and add the following ingredients tied in a cloth: 2 oz. of sweet basil, 2 oz. of marjoram, 1 oz. of sage, 1 oz. of thyme, 18 cloves, 12 bay-leaves, and the peel of 1 lemon.

Let the soup simmer for two or three hours, or until the turtle is cooked; then, with the aid of a skimmer, remove the turtle meat, put it into a basin of cold water, wash it well to free it from all impurities, cut into one-inch square pieces, and lay in a cool place for further use.

Have 10 lbs. of lean beef chopped fine and mix with it 4 whites of eggs and 1 quart of water. Remove all fat from the turtle broth, strain it and add it gradually to the chopped beef; set on the fire to clarify, stirring occasionally to prevent setting on the bottom of the pan; let simmer 1 hour and then strain.

Place the cut turtle meat in saucepan, add the strained broth, set on the range and let boil for 15 minutes.

The soup needs now but the finishing touch—that is, the necessary quantity of cayenne and about 1 quart of good sherry (or more, according to taste—though too much wine is injurious to the flavour).

GREEN TURTLE SOUP, CLEAR À LA ROYAL OR
THICK WITH MARROW QUENELLES

Clear.—Put eight quarts of beef stock into a soup-pot with four pounds of leg of veal, and four pounds of fowl or chicken wings, thyme, bay leaf, parsley, basil, marjoram, mushroom trimmings, and celery; boil all for three hours, then strain through a sieve, and afterward through a napkin. Clarify this stock the same as consommé with chopped beef. Cook separately the prepared turtle, and keep it warm in a steamer (bain-marie); add to the soup a dessertspoonful of arrowroot for each quart, diluted with a little water, and add it to the boiling broth, stirring it in with a whip; boil and despumate the soup for twenty minutes, then season. When ready to serve, drain the turtle, lay it in a soup tureen, and pour over the stock, seasoning with cayenne pepper and a half a gill of Xères for each quart.

For Clear Turtle à la Royal—Add some royale timbales (No. 241).

Thick Turtle with Marrow Quenelles.—Proceed exactly the same as for clear turtle, but instead of thickening it with arrowroot, thicken the soup with a little brown roux, moistened with the turtle stock, boil and despumate, and strain through a fine sieve. Garnish with marrow quenelles (No. 252), or if preferred, use turtle fat instead of marrow. Quenelles may also be made with a quarter of a pound of hard boiled egg yolks pounded with one ounce of butter and four raw egg yolks, seasoning with salt, nutmeg, and chopped parsley; divide this into pieces, roll them into balls a half an inch in diameter, and poach them in boiling water; drain, and serve with the soup.

Poached Eggs au Gratin

This recipe was published in the January 31, 1894 edition of *La Cuisine Française et Etrangère*, one of three recipes Monsieur Colombié, chef and vice-president of the Academy of Cuisine, demonstrated as part of a class on January 15 of the same year. The introduction says that participants came from all over Paris, but "above all the aristocratic neighborhoods."

To poach the eggs, preferably small in size from young hens, lay them in a casserole that has three liters of water with two shot glasses of vinegar or the juice of a lemon. Take note that it is not necessary to salt the water, just add the vinegar, because it acts as an astringent for the albumin in the egg, whereas the salt acts as a dissolvent. When the water begins to boil, you break eight eggs, one at a time, onto a plate and slide them into the boiling water; bring the water back to the boil and then place the pot at the back of the stove, and leave covered for two minutes. Spread a linen towel folded in half on the table; with a spoon or preferably a copper skimmer take the eggs out one by one and place them on the towel.

Moreover, you need to prepare a Béchamel sauce by melting 30–40 grams of butter in a small casserole, mix in a small spoon of fine wheat flour; a pinch of nutmeg and ground white pepper, a little salt, pour in a liter of scalded milk and stir quickly (the milk can easily curdle), the sauce will thicken; add 50 grams of grated cheese, parmesan, gruyère, or the two combined; lightly butter a silver or enameled platter; pour onto it a little sauce, spread it out and arrange the poached eggs, seven around the edge and one in the middle; cover the eggs with the rest of the sauce, sprinkle with more grated cheese. Many people choose gruyère which has a reputation for being the best, but that is a mistaken presumption.

Slide the plate into the oven so that the plate receives a lot of heat on top, but very little on the bottom, you can elevate the plate on top of a cold brick or a casserole which has cold water inside.

It is not necessary to put butter underneath the cheese as many cooks do; the butter melts the cheese, and this often creates places that burn rather than gratiné.

When the plate is equally golden on the surface, remove and serve.

Notes

Introduction

Haute cuisine in the broadest sense simply differentiates types of food practices within a territorially bounded population: a direct connection exists between the type of food prepared and the social and economic status of the desirous consumer. Within any geographic locale, complexities of social organization reveal themselves in food preparation and consumption. For example, in France during the medieval period, the peasantry subsisted chiefly on bread. Though of France, their food had no real resemblance to French haute cuisine. During any day in a given geographic region, all the residents will eat food, but not always the same food or the same style of preparation. My inquiry into the foodways of a certain place and time begins with these questions: What *type* of food am I examining? What *sort* of person consumes it? Why? Sidney Mintz's definition of haute cuisine provides an excellent tool for imposing order on the otherwise immense category of food. His complete definition is the following: "Along what lines can the haute cuisine of a class or privileged group reveal its 'hauteness'? By what it cooks and serves—nightingale tongues and caviar—sometimes ensured by sumptuary distinctions (only the kings get to eat swans and sturgeons). By supplying things out of season—the first fruits, only the best at the season's height, the last available. . . . By how it cooks—number of person hours and quantities of accumulated skills (often as functions of each other) invested in each mouthful" ("Cuisine and Haute Cuisine," 186). For Mintz, the hauteness of a cuisine lies in the way it marks the elite status of the consumers. However, because the exclusive nature of haute cuisine extends to those who make it, I would add two other elements to his definition: the identity of those who cook and serve, and the expertise that makes the cooks masters of hauteness.

1. Cointreau, introduction, *Le Cordon Bleu at Home*, ix.
2. Interestingly, French chefs became much less involved with the American Culinary Federation after World War II, and the organization came to be dominated by German, Swiss, Austrian, and native-born American chefs. Despite the change in the nationality of its membership, the main culinary principles and values espoused remained French.

3. In 1998 the annual banquet was held at the New England Culinary Institute in Vermont. The menu (elegantly printed in both French and English) included squab consommé and roasted rack of veal. From observer accounts, the highlight of the evening was the presentation of individual servings of granité, each served atop a chef's toque, carved out of ice and lit from within by a sparkler. Replicas of the Maître Cuisiniers de France medallions made of chocolate were also presented to the guests.

4. Ohnuki-Tierney, introduction, *Culture Through Time*. Following Foucault, anthropologists now argue that culture can best be analyzed when studies are framed as "genealogies of the present." See Appadurai, "Global Ethnoscapes"; Gupta and Ferguson, "Beyond 'Culture'"; Hannerz, "Cosmopolitans and Locals in World Culture."

5. Mintz, "Cuisine and Haute Cuisine," 186–90. In this article, Mintz discusses the distinction made between "high" and "low" cuisine in Goody's *Cooking, Cuisine, and Class*.

6. Mennell, *All Manners of Food*, 1.

7. Cosman, *Fabulous Feasts*, 33.

8. Mennell, *All Manners of Food*, 56–61.

9. Scully, ed., *Viandier of Taillevent*, 25.

10. Ibid., 21–23.

11. Ibid., 283.

12. Ibid., 288.

13. Henisch, *Fast and Feast*, 101. The quotation is from Richard Warner, *Antiquitates Culinariae* (1791), xxxii.

14. Ibid., 23.

15. Wilson, "Ritual, Form and Color," 25.

16. Laurioux, "Spices in the Medieval Diet," 45.

17. Ibid., 53. Laurioux states that ginger, cinnamon, and pepper appear to have been the most commonly used of the spices and the most prevalent in commercial sources.

18. Scully, ed., *Viandier of Taillevent*, 24.

19. Elias, *The Civilizing Process*.

20. Wheaton, *Savoring the Past*, 115.

21. Ibid., 116.

22. Marin, *Les Dons de Comus*, xxiv.

23. Ibid.

24. Ibid., vj.

25. Carême, *Le Cuisinier Pratique*, 16.

26. Ibid., 146.

Chapter 1. The Cuisine

Cookbooks both disseminate and preserve culinary knowledge. For the authors, these books communicate their understanding of culinary practices. Cookbooks, primarily utilitarian manuals, also reveal much about the author and audience. What knowledge is assumed? Promoted? For haute cuisine the professional chef's stance toward his audience affects the overall execution of his cookbook; his tone and information vary depending on the reader, whether a colleague or housewife. Cookbooks cannot be overlooked in the search for professional cuisine, and in fact are the texts most often used by culinary historians, since they usually include all the requisite materials for analyzing a cuisine: ingredients, method, technique, and presentation.

They also come to function as a fundamental vehicle for the transmission of knowledge, and thus their content has tremendous significance to culinary practice. The information, the strategies, and the recommendation contained within the discourse has power only when the words have been transformed into objects of consumption. The written word helped chefs move from anonymous domestics in the homes of the nobility to experts for the public because now their knowledge could go anywhere. This culinary discourse became a transnational and transhistorical discourse and ultimately defined cooking practices in the Western world. In this context, French haute cuisine became a transportable good and thus capable of tremendous impact. There were two modes of transport for French haute cuisine: one, via textual forms such as cookbooks and journals, and two, via French chefs. Bourgeois cuisine, always associated with the home, did not travel as early or as far, because it was not necessarily associated with expertise. Jean-François Revel argues that French chefs were vital to the ongoing development of what he calls an "international Grand cuisine" which began to flourish after the French Revolution and had its heyday from 1870 to 1920. In his definition of this cuisine, ultimately a cuisine that transcends national boundaries, he argues that "Grand cuisine is a cuisine restricted to professionals."

Regardless of national identity, modern chefs have an ongoing respect for French haute cuisine in the realm of technique and method. As the chefs at the Cordon Bleu in London said to me repeatedly, "You need to know the basics, and that is French technique and method." In cooking schools, in restaurants, and in hotels, the idea that professional standards have a cultural derivation has long been disseminated. The equation of standard professional knowledge and French haute cuisine continues in the contemporary milieu: this association is a fundamental assumption used by those involved in culinary practice to explain the form and content of their labor.

1. Wheaton, *Savoring the Past*, 33.
2. Ibid., 113.
3. Willan, *Great Cooks*, 53.
4. Gouffé, *Livre de Cuisine*, ii.
5. The shift from singular, Ménage, to plural, Ménages, is true to the text.
6. Gouffé, *Livre de Cuisine*, ii.
7. Escoffier, *Escoffier Cookbook*, 1.
8. Child et al., *Mastering the Art of French Cooking*, 1:55.
9. Escoffier, *Escoffier Cookbook*, 2.
10. The classic method of clarifying stock is to filter the liquid through a sieve containing whipped egg whites, the foam functioning to trap even the smallest impurities.
11. Escoffier, *Escoffier Cookbook*, 11.
12. Marin, *Les Dons de Comus*, 1.
13. Dumas, *Dumas on Food*, 74–75.
14. Escoffier, *Escoffier Cookbook*, 13.
15. Simon, *Concise Encyclopedia of Gastronomy*, 25.
16. Escoffier, *Escoffier Cookbook*, 13.
17. Montagné, *La Grande Cuisine Illustrée*, 506.
18. Saulnier, *Répertoire de la Cuisine*, 20.
19. Escoffier, *Escoffier Cookbook*, 364.
20. Dubois, *Cuisine de Tous les Pays*. On the bottom of this menu, there is the line "Diner servi par M. Loucheux." It is my guess that is the name of the chef de cuisine of the grand duchess.

21. Escoffier, *Escoffier Cookbook*, 24.
22. Child et al., *Mastering the Art of French Cooking*, 1:55.
23. Escoffier, *Escoffier Cookbook*, 59.
24. Andrews, "Girardet After Girardet," 103.
25. Deliée, *Franco-American Cookery Book*.
26. Wells and Rubochon, *Simply French*, 143.
27. Escoffier, *Escoffier Cookbook*, 201.
28. Archive of hotel menus, Schlesinger Library.
29. Garrett, *Encyclopedia of Practical Cookery*, 230–40.
30. David, *French Provincial Cooking*, 198.
31. Child et al., *Mastering the Art of French Cooking*, 13. The final statement is definitely true of the modern kitchen—domestic or professional—with the development of ready heat sources such as gas and electricity.
32. Ibid.
33. Guérard, *Cuisine Minceur*, 29.
34. Brillat-Savarin, *Physiology of Taste*, 4.
35. Escoffier, *Escoffier Cookbook*, 117–18.
36. See Escoffier, *Escoffier Cookbook;* Saint-Ange, *Cuisine de Madame Saint-Ange*.
37. Saint-Ange, *Cuisine de Madame Saint-Ange*, 43.
38. Montagné, *Larousse Gastronomique*, 334.
39. Pépin, *La Technique*, 239.
40. Dumas, *Dumas on Food*, 243–44.
41. Child et al., *Mastering the Art of French Cooking*, 11.
42. Dubois, *Cuisine de Tous les Pays*, 20.
43. Saint Ange, *Cuisine de Madame Saint Ange*, 34.
44. Scully, ed., *Viandier de Taillevent*, 3.
45. Escoffier, *Auguste Escoffier*, 118.
46. Ibid., 118–20.
47. Escoffier, *Escoffier Cookbook*, 94.
48. Ibid., 93.
49. Ibid., 266–67.
50. Distel, *Cuisine Pratique*, 1.
51. Ibid., 2.
52. Ibid., 15.

Chapter 2. The Emergence of the Restaurant

Haute cuisine persists despite the transformations in the organization of French society by the early 1800s. The need to assert and preserve "hauteness" continues, but the locations shift. There is a transition from the domestic sphere of the nobility to the public sphere of elites and bourgeoisie in France as the primary locale for French haute cuisine, be it production or consumption. By following the cuisine and the people dedicated to its execution, the persistence of social hierarchy (despite the move to democracy) can be traced, while the new signs and symbols that mark "status" are revealed. As well, with the turn from the eighteenth to the nineteenth century came a fairly dramatic chain of events in the world of professional food production in France and England. Chefs, formerly working in noble households, were now able, in a sense, to hang out their own shingles in this array of public locales. After the Revolution, democracy did arrive for culinary producers: they now had choices as to where they could work—restaurants, noble homes, clubs, or hotels.

1. La Varenne, *Cuisinier Français*.
2. Monselet, *Le Gourmet: Journal des Intérêts Gastronomiques* 1, no. 1 (February 21, 1858).
3. Wheaton, *Savoring the Past*, 76. The quotation is from *Relations des Ambassadeurs Venitiens sur les Affaires de France au XVIème Siècle*, ed. and trans. Niccolò Tommaseo, 1838, 603.
4. Chaucer, *Canterbury Tales*, 137. In this Penguin edition the Tales are translated into modern English by Neville Coghill.
5. Ibid., 137.
6. Clough, *Economic History of Europe*, 27.
7. Ibid., 29.
8. Jones, *Butchers of London*, 1. Thrupp, in *Short History*, puts the date of official recognition of the company sometime between 1130 and 1155 and rightly points out that this means, "not that the bakers first organized in 1155, but that by that date they were strong enough to strike a bargain with the officials of the Exchequer," 2.
9. Herbage, *History of the Worshipful Company of Cooks*, 1.
10. Ibid., 3.
11. Ibid.
12. L'Espinasse, *Métiers de Paris*, vol. 1, 290.
13. These terms may be translated as chef de cuisine, cook, and caterer. There is no scholarly discussion I have been able to find on the portechapper trade.
14. Spang, "Confusion of Appetites," 129.
15. L'Espinasse, *Métiers de Paris*, 300.
16. Wheaton, *Savoring the Past*, 72.
17. Spang, "Confusion of Appetites," 130–34.
18. Thrupp, *Short History*, 56.
19. Ibid., 62.
20. Herbage, *History of the Worshipful Company of Cooks*, 185.
21. Thrupp, *Short History*, 64.
22. Kaplow, *Names of Kings*, 19.
23. Ibid.
24. Ibid., 29.
25. Herbage, *History of the Worshipful Company of Cooks*, 186.
26. Ibid., 187.
27. Spang, "Confusion of Appetites," 130–33.
28. Ibid., 134.
29. Ibid., 160–64.
30. Ibid., 109. Spang argues that restaurateurs made the change in the menu so diners could choose the "restaurants" that would ameliorate their individual maladies.
31. Brillat-Savarin, *Physiology of Taste*, 309. The quotation comes from M. F. K. Fisher's 1949 translation.
32. Ibid., 311.
33. Wheaton, *Savoring the Past*, 77.
34. Revel, *Culture and Cuisine*, 209.
35. "The Growth of the American Restaurant," *The Epicure* (1906), 35.
36. Zeldin, *Taste and Corruption*, 384.
37. Wheaton, *Savoring the Past*.

38. Ibid., 160. Wheaton argues that these chefs did much to spread the principles of French haute cuisine abroad, but that they also introduced preparations learned abroad to their native cuisine.

39. Ibid., 163–65.

40. Toomre, introduction, *Classic Russian Cooking*, 20–21.

41. Spang, *Confusion of Appetites*, 246.

42. Ibid.

43. Favre, *Dictionnaire Universel*, 542.

44. Châtillon-Plessis, *Vie à Table*.

45. Escoffier, *Escoffier Cookbook*, 73.

46. Beauvilliers, *L'Art de Cuisinier*.

47. Brillat-Savarin, *Physiology of Taste*, 315.

48. Escoffier, *Escoffier Cookbook*.

49. Châtillon-Plessis, *Vie à Table*, 311.

50. Revel, *Culture and Cuisine*, 223–24.

51. For an excellent study of the history of commodification of a food crop—sugar—see Mintz, *Sweetness and Power*.

52. Jerrold, *Epicure's Yearbook*, 145.

53. Turning scholarly attention toward practitioners affects the organization and the outcomes of scholarship: the traditional loci for studies on foodways—home and nation—are shifted and an examination of professionals reveals the processes and agency involved in creating a cuisine.

54. Jerrold, *Epicure's Yearbook*, 145.

Chapter 3. The British

Once French haute cuisine makes a move to the public sphere, blocks of anonymous consumers assure its continuance. The consumer comes first because in the public sphere the customer opens all the doors. The newly emerging public sphere in England creates a broader set of dining options and a larger set of potential consumers. The British consumer facilitates an understanding of the international appeal of France's cuisine. In order for the knowledge of French haute cuisine, the necessary ideas and skills, to have survived over three centuries, there must have been people interested in savoring the products of the masters of French cuisine, since without demand there is no reason for such knowledge to flourish. The case of cuisine also shows the importance of the producers of commodities in the ability of objects, values, and practices to move beyond place of origin.

1. Mennell, *All Manners of Food*, 207.

2. Girouard, *Victorian Pubs*, 26.

3. Ibid., 11.

4. Ibid., 6.

5. "Clubs of Old," 1–4.

6. Ibid., 3.

7. Ibid., 2.

8. "Club Life," 1.

9. Mackenzie, *The Savoy Hotel*, 52.

10. Whitton, "Clubbable Man."

11. Favre, *Dictionnaire Universel de Cuisine Pratique*, 119. Ude also published *The French Cook; or the Art of Cookery Developed in All Branches* (1813).

12. Woodbridge, *The Reform Club*.

13. Ibid.

14. Beard, in the introduction to *Soyer's Cookery Book*, vii.

15. Soyer, *Memoirs of Soyer*, 6.

16. For example, in 1846 Soyer prepared a grand banquet for 150 people at the Reform Club held in honor of the Ibrahim Pasha of Egypt. The banquet presented over two hundred dishes, including turbot, sauce à la Mazarin, poussins printaniers à l'ambassadrice, and gâteau Britannique à l'amiral.

17. Archives, Reform Club. Translation: turtle soup, quail in a cold sauce, saddle of lamb with a red currant sauce, roast pheasant, and a coffee parfait.

18. Ibid. Translation: clear consommé, lamb chops, roast pheasant.

19. "Les Restaurants Anglais," xiv.

20. Ibid., 7.

21. "Cuisine Française en Angleterre," iii. In this context my intentions are literal; all the people under discussion are French, and there is every indication that they were all French citizens.

22. Ibid.

23. Editorial, *Food and Cookery and the Catering World*.

24. Neirinck and Poulain, *Histoire de la Cuisine et des Cuisiniers*, 90–91.

25. Mackenzie, *Savoy of London*, 39.

26. Ibid., 52.

27. Ibid., 53. Mackenzie goes on to state that English cooking "was not to be ignored," and that cuisines of other nations could also be ordered, especially the popular dishes of the United States: canvasback duck, terrapin, clams, and sweet corn. D'Oyly Carte knew there was a large market of wealthy Americans that he would need to satisfy.

28. Escoffier, *Souvenirs Inédits*, 99.

29. Ritz, *César Ritz*, 122.

30. Mennell, *All Manners of Food*, 159.

31. Escoffier, *Souvenirs Inédits*, 101.

32. Ritz, *César Ritz*.

33. The bourgeoisie were not the only class group socializing in new public locales during the second half of the nineteenth century. Roy Rosenzweig documents the rise of the working-man's saloon in America, particularly Worcester and Boston, during this period. Saloons were the domain of the working class; the "rich scions of nobility" would drink and socialize at home, in clubs, or at hotels ("The Rise of the Saloon," 121). He attributes the rising importance of the saloon in social life to long-term transformations in the organization of society: "the separation of work and play, the segregation of recreation from home life, and the commercialization of this leisure time and space" (156). These changes involved all members of society, but, as Rosenzweig rightly points out, their specific manifestations, in this case sociality that was both public and commercial in nature, were class specific.

34. Douglas, "Goods as a System of Communication," 29.

35. This may not be the case in the contemporary period; when I was in France in 1993, such three-star chefs as Paul Bocuse and Michel Guérard were involved in the production of frozen and pre-packaged gourmet foods.

36. Appadurai, *Social Life of Things*.
37. Ibid., 15.

Chapter 4. Cultural Nationalism

How were decisions about *quality* of food made during the nineteenth century? Questions of quality came to be answered differently for consumers and producers of food. For British consumers of French haute cuisine, questions of quality become translated into concerns about having good taste, desires to participate in elite culture, and the ability to discern what makes some food fancy and some food plain.

For the producers, questions of quality become transformed into concerns about "skill" and "mastery." And all these issues—taste, culture, discernment, skill, mastery— became associated with French haute cuisine. Distinction, therefore, in the realm of fancy food possesses a powerful cultural dimension. This is true for both producers and consumers of French cuisine, because "French cuisine has long enjoyed a preeminent reputation among the cuisines of the world; continuing dominance of the culinary world order is a matter of national pride" (Terrio, "Crafting *Grand Cru* Chocolates," 70). Thus the historical link between professional chefs and French haute cuisine emerges partly as a result of the shift of the practice into the public sphere at a moment in Europe's history when France, the nation, dominated as France, the culture. By 1895, when the British patron at a fine dining establishment such as the Carlton Hotel sat down to filets de sole Véronique, he consumed culture as well as a piece of fish.

This chapter critically considers the way "culture" has been assumed in contemporary anthropological literature with a look at historical definitions of the same term. Nineteenth-century informants reveal a more refracted version of culture than traditionally considered in anthropology, mediated through class and gender. Bourgeois consumers of haute cuisine in London and Paris had a more unified vision of "elite culture" than any vision they shared with other fellow citizens. This approach queries the objectivist and empiricist tendencies of anthropology's "quest for the present," under disciplinary scrutiny for some time. An alternative method often suggested is to create a more historical picture of present situations, what Arjun Appadurai calls "genealogies of the present."

1. Kirwan, *Host and Guest*, 61 (emphasis mine).
2. I am using a very broad brush here in my discussion of nineteenth-century Europe. No detailed historical work has been done on French haute cuisine during the first half of the century. What has been done sweeps through the entire century and thus a certain level of detail is lost. At the same time, French haute cuisine during the entire span of the nineteenth century (the types of dishes being made and consumed) is characterized by continuity rather than change.
3. In locales outside France up through today, menus often use the term "Continental cuisine" to describe certain types of dishes. The signification changes from place to place. In India it generally indicates "Western" dishes; in England it generally indicates French dishes. By the same token, in England during the nineteenth century restaurants and hotels would often advertise that there was a "Continental chef" in the kitchen. These men were not necessarily native-born Frenchmen but men from Italy, Germany, and Switzerland who had trained either in France or under Frenchmen.
4. See Nord, *Paris Shopkeepers*; Miller, *Bon Marché*; Bowlby, *Just Looking*; Auslander, *The Creation of Value*.

5. James, "Occasional Paris," 115.

6. Edel, *Henry James*.

7. Helm, *Ulysses' Sail*.

8. Numerous critiques of the presumptions of ethnography as *the* anthropological genre have appeared, most of which argue that it should be seen as a constructed rather than reported form of documentation. (For examples, see Clifford and Marcus, *Writing Culture*; Marcus and Fischer, *Anthropology as Cultural Critique*; Fox, ed., *Recapturing Anthropology*.)

9. From *The Letters of Samuel Johnson*, found in Ousby, *Englishman's England*, 9.

10. Handler, "High Culture, Hegemony, and Historical Causality," 818.

11. Theodore Zeldin states: "The first and most influential theory about France was that it stood for 'civilization.' To be a Frenchman, in the fullest sense, meant to be civilized, which required that one accepted the models of thought, behaviour and expression held in esteem in Paris. . . . By this definition, to be a Frenchman meant more than to be born in France, or to be a mere peasant; it involved adherence to a set of values, but in return one could hope to benefit from all the rewards that the state showered on those who adopted these values." *France, 1848–1915: Intellect and Pride*, 6.

12. Noel-Waldteufel, "Manger à la Cour," 75.

13. Brulon, "Les Services de Porcelaine de Sèvres," 184.

14. Léonor d'Orey, "L'Histoire des Services d'Orfèvrerie Française à la Cour du Portugal," 165.

15. Ibid., 6.

16. Greenhalgh, *Ephemeral Vistas*, 205.

17. Ibid., 211.

18. Meadab, *Clark's Pocket Paris*, 32.

19. Altick, *English Common Reader*, 355, 396.

20. Newnham-Davis, *Dinners and Diners*.

21. According to Ousby, "the full term 'guidebook' was not . . . coined until the early 19th century, . . . but the concept of guidebook and the colloquialism 'guide,' as well as the cognate 'companion' are creations of the 18th century." *Englishman's England*, 12.

22. Ibid.

23. It is interesting to note the subtle sexism in the final line. The implication appears to be that in Paris men would never let women sway their decisions in the realm of the proper meal.

24. Newnham-Davis, *Gourmet Guide to Europe*, 1.

25. Meadab, *Clark's Pocket Paris*, 102.

26. Francatelli, *Modern Cook*.

27. DeSalis, *Art of Cookery*, 22.

28. Ibid., 25.

29. Jerrold, *Epicure's Yearbook*, 11.

30. Elias, *Civilizing Process*, 3.

31. Williams, *Keywords*, 47.

32. Marx and Engels, "Communist Manifesto," 473.

33. Ibid., 474.

34. Bedarida, *Social History of England*. By the mid-nineteenth century the organization of society in England was based on the capitalist division of labor, and class society

"reached its zenith" between 1880 and 1914 (Perkin, *Rise of Professional Society*, 27). "An examination of the distribution of national income is striking because such a small percentage of the population actually comprises the upper and middle classes—in 1867 a little less than 2 percent (approximately 1,197,000), and in 1904 not more than 8 percent (approximately 3,225,000). In the 1904 calculations, 88.4 percent of the British (English and Welsh) population lived in poverty, meaning that these people did not make enough money to pay income taxes. This vast percentage of the population was in command of only 51.5 percent of the national income" (Perkin, 29–30).

35. Ibid., 63.

36. This quotation is from Beatrice Webb, as found in Perkin, *Rise of Professional Society*, 65.

37. Turner, "Review Article," 159.

38. The other, dark side of the British bourgeois demand for certain types of food and drink is the fact that much of the British imperialist enterprise involved creating appropriate environments where the necessary raw ingredients for many French dishes could be produced. The imperial stance toward its colonies was often articulated in terms of their role as producers for consumers at home, in England.

39. Glasse, *Art of Cookery*, 4.

40. Strong, *Where and How to Dine in Paris*, 5.

41. "French and English Cookery Compared," 135.

42. Briggs, *Social History of England*, 283.

43. Anderson, *Imagined Communities*, 13.

44. I do not mean to imply that all Englishmen, from northern miners to London barristers, were happily consuming French haute cuisine during this period. Everyday eating habits stayed very much the same, varying according to region and access to resources. An English person who *chose* to eat a fine meal, however, ate French.

45. Said, *Culture and Imperialism*.

Chapter 5. Apostles of Hauteness

After French haute cuisine shifted into the public sphere, social hierarchy continued to be mediated symbolically through its dishes, but now the symbols are significant for both consumers and producers. For patrons at the grand restaurants, the food appears at the table as a glorious aesthetic object and an opportunity for sensual pleasure. For the producers, each dish represents their personal mastery and fragile professional identity. Chefs were not alone in their concerns: power in terms of knowledge was vital to the struggle for professional and class identity that began in the nineteenth century and continues to characterize and preoccupy modern society. (The social historian Harold Perkin has documented the importance of professionalism in *The Rise of Professional Society: England Since 1880*.) It is important to look at the main figures in the development of the modern culinary profession and their promotional methods. Turning the scholarly gaze toward practitioners affects the organization and outcomes of scholarship: the traditional loci for studies on foodways—home and nation—are shifted, and an examination of professionals reveals the processes and agency involved in creating a cuisine.

Reading the culinary texts of the late 1800s, an intriguingly small number of people appear to be involved in their production. In *L'Art Cuisinier*, the official publication of the Société des Cuisiniers Français, names of culinary figures such as Fulbert-Dumonteil, Châtillon-Plessis, Escoffier, and Colombié appear repeatedly. These men were also responsible for publishing a variety of other cookbooks, manuals, and gastronomic treatises now axiomatic in the discourse on French haute cuisine. Institution builders as well, they were actively involved in lobbying for a state-sponsored cooking school. These were the founding fathers of the modern culinary profession. In the same manner as ethnographic interviews have long been used, an in-depth analysis of the writings of these French chefs provides an opportunity to understand the wider cultural assumptions that shaped their beliefs and actions. Borrowing from Benedict Anderson's seminal idea about the relationship between print capitalism and national identity during the nineteenth century, these journals create an "imagined community" of like-minded readers, some in search of a social identity, some in search of a professional one.

Nationalism, understood in this context in terms of both practice and identity, informs much of the story, though, as will become clear, nationalistic confidence allows for imperialistic tendencies as well. Chefs often use the rhetoric of imperialism. Clearly they were never truly imperial rulers, for they had no institutionalized power or mechanisms of control. Rather, they were capitalizing on the widespread perception that French haute cuisine defined fine food more generally. The perceived superiority of French haute cuisine by both producer and consumer allowed the French to dominate the highest strata of the culinary world. Looking at both author and audience allows us to paint a portrait of broad cultural concerns as well as the preoccupations of a group of people who shaped the future of professional culinary practice.

1. "Evolution in French Cookery," n.p.
2. The reach of French chefs into the heart of Italian elite culture is particularly interesting, given the ongoing debate in culinary history as to whether the "original location" of French haute cuisine was the Renaissance Italian court. It has been suggested that the cooks Catherine de Medici brought with her to France on her marriage to Henry II in 1533 provided the skill and information that spawned the seventeenth- and eighteenth-century development of French haute cuisine. This story has been questioned by culinary historians as being primarily apocryphal (see Mennell, *All Manners of Foods*, and Wheaton, *Savoring the Past*). It would be impossible for several cooks in one kitchen to be able to generate the changes that occurred in French haute cuisine during that period. Even if it were true, it appears that by the 1800s the French were able to exert or reexert their influence on elite food consumption in Italy. The nineteenth-century information comes from "Rome Gourmand," *L'Art Culinaire*, September 1892.
3. Ludden, "Orientalist Empiricism," 251, calls this "epistemological authority."
4. Editorial, *Food and Cookery and Catering World*, 29.
5. "Tout est Dans Tout," 135. The original French is as follows: "La Cuisine est un art. C'est même un art éminemment français, en ce double sens: 1 que nulle part il n'a été poussé au même degré de raffinement que dans la patrie de Vatel et de Brillat-Savarin; 2 que presque partout (dans les pays civilisés), le scepter est en généralement tenu par les mains françaises." Vatel was the maître d'hôtel for members of the nobility in the era of Louis XIV.
6. See Foucault, *Power/Knowledge*; Comaroff and Comaroff, *Of Revelation and Revolution*.
7. The original French is "Les Français se glorifiant de voir le goût de leur cuisine

regner, avec le même empire que leur langue et leur modes, sur les états opulents de l'Europe, du nord au midi."

8. Gilbert, "Cuisine Français," 42 (original emphasis).

9. See Guha and Spivak, *Subaltern Studies*; Comaroff and Comaroff, *Of Revelation and Revolution*.

10. Guha, "Some Aspects of Historiography of Colonial India," 38–42.

11. "The Art of the Paris Chef," 2 (emphasis added). There is another form of irony in this excerpt. Cooking may be characterized as the French industry, but America was a place where industrialized food production and packaging happened quite early and very successfully. The company that published this magazine, S. S. Pierce, was itself a food packaging company. It also owned the very successful A&P chain of grocery stores.

12. Rosalind Williams, "Dream World," 231.

13. Escoffier, *Escoffier Cookbook*, 15. The exact quotation is as follows: "En ce temps-là, le métier de cuisinier était peu considéré dans la société mondaine. Pourtant cela n'aurait pas dû être le cas, car la cuisine est une science et un art, et l'homme qui met tout son coeur à satisfaire son semblable mérite d'être considéré."

14. I have culled biographical information from numerous sources, including *L'Art Culinaire, La Cuisine Française et Etrangère, Cook's Journal*, and *Dictionnaire Universel de Cuisine Pratique*, and created a biographical database of approximately sixty nineteenth-century chefs.

15. Biography of Joseph Favre, included in *Dictionnaire Universel de Cuisine Pratique*.

16. Ibid. Favre's ongoing interest in pursuing higher education is an interesting and probably fairly unusual aspect of his biography.

17. I have not found evidence of other nineteenth-century chefs taking university courses in the course of their careers. The author of the biography I consulted, E. Darenne, was a journalist involved with the culinary profession. He intimates that it was highly unusual for a member of Favre's profession.

18. Ibid.

19. Ibid.,130.

20. Auslander, *Creation of Value*, 159–63.

21. Ibid., 160.

22. Dupeux, *French Society*, 135–38.

23. For more on the *petit commerce* movement, see Nord, *Paris Shopkeepers*, 1986.

24. Given the constricted circumstances most of the aspiring chefs I studied came from, not all of them went to Paris at the beginning of their careers. Some did their initial apprenticeship in cities closer to their homes such as Geneva, Lausanne, or Monte Carlo. But they all eventually spent some time working in Paris.

25. Dupeux, *French Society*, 105.

26. The grand hotels, which had tremendous dining rooms and banquet facilities and thus needed large kitchen staffs, did not become popular until the 1870s. Until that time the kitchens of restaurants and noble homes were the most likely place of employment. Paris also had the advantage of being the headquarters of many of the associations that became increasingly important for workers in the food trades.

27. Tschumi, *Annals of Labour*, 195–98.

28. Tschumi came from Lausanne in French-speaking Switzerland.

29. Franey, *Chef's Tale*, 37.

30. Ibid.

31. Ibid., 47–48.

32. Orwell, *Down and Out in Paris and London*, 57.

33. Tschumi, *Annals of Labour*, 193–94.

34. Orwell, *Down and Out in Paris and London*, 70.

35. Ibid., 76. Orwell also comments on the fact that certain jobs were given to certain nationalities: "The office employees and the cooks and sewing women were French, the waiters Italians and Germans (there is hardly such thing as a French waiter in Paris), the plongeurs of every race [in] Europe, besides Arabs and negroes" (71). This leads me to speculate that more forms of labor than cooking came to have national identities attached to them in this period.

36. Dupeux, *French Society*, 116.

37. Husson, *Consommations de Paris*, 72.

38. "Portraits of Great Chefs," 10.

39. "Rome Gourmande," xix.

40. Favre, *Dictionnaire Universel de Cuisine Pratique*.

41. Nord, *Paris Shopkeepers*, 46–47; emphasis added.

42. Ibid., 68. Potin manufactured preserves, condiments, and chocolate among other things.

43. Ibid., 89.

44. Some of the associations were the Société de Secours Mutuels des Pâtissiers-Glaciers, Société des Secours Mutuels des Cuisiniers, Société des Garçons de Salle, Société des Artistes Culinaires de Paris, Chambre Syndicale des Cuisiniers-Pâtissiers de Paris, Société des Cuisiniers Français, Union Universelle pour le Progrès de l'Art Culinaire, Les Amis de Saint Laurent, La Persévérance, L'Académie de Cuisine. Some of the journals were *La Cuisine Française et Etrangère*, *Le Journal des Confiseurs-Pâtissiers*, *Le Journal des Confiseurs, Pâtissiers, Glaciers*, *L'Etoile*, *Le Progrès des Cuisiniers*, *L'Art Culinaire*, *Le Gourmet*, *Le Cordon Bleu*, *Le Pot au Feu*, and *La Bonne Cuisine*.

45. Favre, *Dictionnaire Universel de Cuisine Pratique*, xv.

46. Bowlby, *Just Looking*, 85–86.

47. Dupeux, *French Society*.

48. Altick, *English Common Reader*, 171.

49. There has not been much exploration of these sources so far by historians. Culinary historians have tended to examine cookbooks in their research on food values and practices of a certain time and place. Mennell, in *All Manners of Food*, does examine several journals, but he doesn't consider the structure and content of this genre to constitute a separate body of information.

50. Monselet also published a small book entitled *Almanach des Gourmands* in 1862. Probably intended as a reference guide for eating in Paris, the subtitle is *Archives Gastronomiques, Recettes, Menus de Saison, Guide du Diner, Conseiller des Estomacs, Dialogues de Table, Variétés Apéritives, Poésies Relevées, etc.*

51. One 1897 cookbook, in fact, is called *Traité Pratique de Cuisine Bourgeoise Faisant Suite aux Eléments Culinaires à l'Usage des Jeune Filles.*

52. "Exposition Culinaire," 77.

53. I am borrowing Benedict Anderson's seminal idea about the relationship between print capitalism and national identity during the nineteenth century.

54. "French Cookery," 37.

Chapter 6. Schools, Standards, and Status

This chapter looks at the rising structural and symbolic importance overall of the professions during the late nineteenth century and the attempts of chefs to become players in this new organization of production. Chefs were engaged in the professionalizing process. Both sociologists and historians concur that *professional* organizations emerge in the nineteenth century, and that their power solidifies in Europe after 1870. The historian Harold Perkin states, "Where pre-industrial society was based on passive property in land and industrial society on actively managed capital, *professional society is based on human capital created by education and enhanced by strategies of closure, that is, the exclusion of the unqualified*" (*Rise of Professional Society*, 2; emphasis mine). In the case of cooking, the expert knowledge deemed necessary to attain professional status is understood within the profession to consist of certain technical skills. As haute cuisine moved farther afield, to the streets of London, New York, and even Rome, French chefs wanted to ensure that *all* people making fine food in the public sphere would be French, or would at least thoroughly master the principles of French haute cuisine, in an attempt to create such closure.

The informants, chefs of the period, were deeply committed to the notion of a culinary *profession*. A substantial portion of the scholarly literature on the structure and organization of the professions considers the importance of group centrality versus group marginality in the development of the professions. This literature ranges from abstract theoretical formulations that explicate the criteria necessary for a labor form to be truly a profession to microhistorical studies of the changing shape of one of these professions in a particular time and place. These studies depend on one another for conceptual frameworks and historical details.

Eliot Friedson and Magali Sarfatti Larson have developed sociological theories that use continuities between groups that have historically succeeded in their attempts to professionalize. They make a distinction between a generalized rhetoric of professionalism and a more specific ability to obtain or guarantee certain claims for particular organizational groups. In this type of argument it is considered that origins and outcomes involve different spheres of analysis. Ultimately, chefs were never able to obtain those claims. There were limits to how far the "hauteness" of their practice would take them in the organization of occupations. The consideration of chefs' aims brings the shape and rationale of haute cuisine into sharper relief than found in traditional culinary studies.

1. Williams, *Country and the City*, 304–5.
2. Reader, *Professional Men*, 9.
3. Ibid., 10.
4. Weiss, "Bridges and Barriers."
5. Barberet, *Travail en France*, 4.
6. Châtillon-Plessis, "Chronique Professionnelle," 126.
7. *Conseil Municipal de la Ville de Paris: Rapports et Documents*, 1890, 143: 6–9. The complete list of schools being supported by the Conseil Municipal is as follows: L'Ecole Municipale de Physique et Chimie Industrielles, L'Ecole Professionnelle d'Ameublement, L'Ecole Estienne (de former des ouvriers habiles et instruits pour les arts et industries du livre), L'Ecole Professionnelle et Ménagère de Filles, L'Ecole Professionnelle de la Rue Fonday, Ecole Professionnelle de la Rue Bouret, Ecole Professionnelle de la Rue Bousselet, Ecole Professionnelle de la Rue Gameron, Ecole Professionnelle de la Rue de Poitou (couture, mâche, broderie, dessin et peinture; cours commerciaux), and Ecole Professionnelle de la Rue de la Tome-Issoie.

8. Auslander, "Creation of Value," 159–63.
9. The Conseil de Prud'hommes was created to monitor employer-employee relations and arbitrate disputes.
10. Châtillon-Plessis, "Chronique Professionnelle," 78.
11. Châtillon-Plessis, *Vie à Table*, 214–15.
12. Hobsbawm, *Age of Empire*.
13. Ibid., 119.
14. Perkin, *Rise of Professional Society*, 3.
15. Delahaire, *Historique Sommaire*, n.p.
16. These books were *Cuisine Artistique, Etudes de l'Ecole Moderne, La Cuisine d'Aujourd'hui: Ecole des jeunes Cuisiniers, La Cuisine de Tous les Pays, Etudes Cosmopolites, Ecole des Cuisinières*, and *La Cuisine Classique* with Emile Bernard.
17. *L'Art Culinaire*, 2–3.
18. Ibid.
19. Ozanne, "Deux Jours à Londres," 125–26.
20. *Universal Food and Cookery Annual*, 77.
21. Barberet, *Travail en France*.
22. "La Mutualité," 1.
23. Dupeux, *French Society, 1789–1970*.
24. Barberet, *Travail en France*, 72.
25. Ibid.
26. "Placement Gratuit des Ouvriers Pâtissiers-Cuisiniers," 1.
27. Virmaître, *Progrès Gastronomique*.
28. I think this is especially the case when you consider the journal as a written text. The journal is the most efficient way to promote and disseminate this knowledge—it can serve as a sort of cookbook as well as an association journal.
29. Editorial, "Progrès de la Chambre Syndicale des Cuisiniers de Paris," 3.
30. Ibid.
31. Gilbert, "L'Arbitrage." Philéas Gilbert was also a frequent contributor to *L'Art Culinaire* and appears to have been extremely active in both the Société des Cuisiniers Français and the Chambre Syndicale des Cuisiniers.
32. "Protestation," 1.
33. Virmaître, "Ecole Pour Cuisiniers à Londres," 2–4.
34. Ibid.
35. Ibid.
36. "Réglement," n.p. As can be seen by the specific areas of education listed above, the "nutritional sciences" component of the school was very much secondary to the culinary arts component.
37. Châtillon-Plessis, *Vie à Table*.
38. Larson, "In the Manner of Experts," 31.
39. Said, *Culture and Imperialism*, 9.
40. For recent studies that look at knowledge and imperialism, see Said, *Culture and Imperialism* and Suleri, *Rhetoric of British India*.

Chapter 7. The Culinary Expositions in Britain and France

The larger, communitarian interests of the parties involved with French haute cuisine, when community is understood to mean social class, shape their perceptions and analyses of haute cooking practice. I focus primarily on the works and writings of chefs and the rhetorical strategies used to create difference (via the process of cooking) out of seeming sameness. In other words, not only did French chefs perceive a difference between hash browns and pommes dauphinoise, they perceived a difference between their pommes dauphinoise and the pommes dauphinoise of the French bourgeois housewife. Difference went far beyond the borders of France. The French chef perceived a real distinction between his pommes dauphinoise and those of the British chef as well. To complicate matters, potatoes in the hands of a French chef were also considered superior and worthy of greater acclaim and cost by British bourgeois consumers.

This chapter also examines women's reactions to French haute cuisine and professional chefs' attitudes toward women. Gender identities play a large part in the unfolding of events as members of the professional culinary world struggle to assert themselves. For example, in the culinary journals I examine, men write the articles, promote the profession, and teach at the cooking schools, but the audience for the journals and schools are primarily women. Escoffier stated that he could not have succeeded if it hadn't been for the ladies, yet he also argued vehemently that women had no place in a professional kitchen. Ironically, the very definition of professional cuisine depends on a differentiation from the domestic sphere, yet women, especially their interest in making "haute" cuisine at home, are pivotal to the status of the cuisine.

Among the people involved in these practices, concerns often revolved around the "place" of the various artists and artisans in the social order. Issues of position were articulated at the level of both producer and consumer.

The discourse concerning cooking as an art must be explored within a certain historical context because that context shapes the category of "art" itself. Concerns of class, gender, aesthetics, and status help define this period. Interestingly, in their writings the culinary commentators do not use context-specific language to discuss the art of cuisine; rather, their discourse relies on *universal* categories of art. Kris L. Hardin, who studies African aesthetics and art, analyzes the universalizing tendency in definitions of art in Europe (and America) and points out that this strategy has profound effects on analysis. Viewing art (understood as "Art") as a universal category can erase the "ways in which aesthetic sensibility has been used as a tool for exclusion" and show how "Art" emerges in "specific political and economic circumstances" (Hardin, *Aesthetics of Action*, 266–67). Therefore the discourse on culinary artistry (here discourse includes texts, events, displays, and products) can be seen as a manifestation of a larger "dialectic between structure and action." The evaluations of culinary artistry outlined in the nineteenth-century discourse—as art, as skill, as edible, as high class, as the domain of the male chef—are the manifestations of such a dialectic. The taste for French haute cuisine, not just in France but beyond, makes sense when understood in the context of the structures, actions, and values of nineteenth-century Europe.

1. Charles Herman Senn in Universal Food and Cookery Association, *Annual Report*, 24.
2. Thanks to Kris Hardin for this insight.
3. Williams, *Keywords*, 40–41.
4. See Auslander, *Creation of Value*; Walton, *France at the Crystal Palace*.
5. Silverman, *Art Nouveau*.
6. Ibid., 210–11.
7. Ibid., 214.

8. Ibid., 12.

9. See Spiro Kostof, editor, *The Architect*, 1977.

10. Ibid.

11. Silverman, *Art Nouveau*, 54.

12. Archives Nationales, 1913 Culinary Exposition, n.p. Pellaprat worked for Le Cordon Bleu as a chef-instructor and also published *Le Cuisinier*.

13. Ibid.

14. Ibid.

15. Saumon à la Humbert Ier, 158–59.

16. David, *French Country Cooking*, 8.

17. Ibid., 92.

18. "L'Exposition Culinaire Artistique de Londres," 10–11.

19. Ibid.

20. Senn, *Souvenir*, 16.

21. In a non-"native" environment, the elision of French haute cuisine with other prevalent definitions of "high" (implicit in the French case) is more apparent.

22. Ibid., 16. Lobsters and crayfish were extremely popular ingredients in nineteenth-century haute cuisine, along with truffles, oysters, and turtles.

23. Ibid., 17.

24. Ibid., 25.

25. Women were involved with the administration of cooking schools in Paris. Mademoiselle Distel was the editor of the Cordon Bleu journal that was the inspiration for the Cordon Bleu cooking school.

26. "L'Exposition Culinaire Artistique de Londres," 10.

27. Ibid., 22.

28. Escoffier, "Why Men Make the Best Cooks," 9.

29. See Sussman, *Culture as History*, xii.

30. Silverman, *Art Nouveau*, 71–73.

31. Sarfatti Larson, *Rise of Professionalism*, 48.

Epilogue

If a contemporary American chef had his way, he would continue to create fine and complicated meals for the sophisticated consumer at a high price. For professional chefs interested in being creative and in making a living, the fact that a restaurant meal under modernity exists as a commodity is not under critique. Rather the role of culture, in defining value and meaning, thus determining what *type* of meal is more or less desirable preoccupies chefs. All things being equal, a chef wants to continue to make fine food for Americans, he just does not want to be constrained by consumption demands and production standards into making only "French" food.

The story of the emergence of professional cuisine may force us to consider that the nation, either as a geographical parameter or conceptual category, is not sufficient for the analysis of cooking and eating practices, given their immense breadth and depth. A reexamination of the seemingly obvious and logical connection between nation and culture raises new issues. Above all, how should nation and cuisine be defined, once their status as objective categories, oblivious to change and manipulation, is questioned?

1. Interview with the author.
2. Miller, interview with the author.
3. Darnton, *Great Cat Massacre.*
4. Thomas, "Sushi Cordon Bleu?"; Chaddock, "Precious Few," 17.
5. Chaddock, "Precious Few," 17.
6. Thomas, "Sushi Cordon Bleu?" 41.
7. Clark, "Thoughts for Food," 32.

BIBLIOGRAPHY

Abbott, Andrew. *The System of Professions: An Essay on the Division of Expert Labor.* Chicago: University of Chicago Press, 1988.

Altick, Richard D. *The English Common Reader: A Social History of the Mass Reading Public, 1800–1900.* Chicago: University of Chicago Press, 1957.

Anderson, Benedict. *Imagined Communities: Reflections on the Origin and Spread of Nationalism.* London: Verso Press, 1983.

Andrews, Colman. "Girardet After Girardet." *Saveur* 29 (September–October 1998): 98–110.

Appadurai, Arjun. *The Social Life of Things: Commodities in Cultural Perspective.* Cambridge: Cambridge University Press, 1986.

———. "How to Make a National Cuisine: Cookbooks in Contemporary India." *Contemporary Studies in Society and History* 30(1) (1988): 3–24.

———. "Disjuncture and Difference in the Global Cultural Economy." *Public Culture* 2(2) (1990): 1–24.

———. "Global Ethnoscapes: Notes and Queries for a Transnational Anthropology." In *Recapturing Anthropology*, ed. Richard Fox. Santa Fe, N.M.: School of American Research Press, 1991.

Aron, Jean-Paul. *The Art of Eating in France: Manners and Menus in the Nineteenth Century.* New York: Harper and Row, 1975.

"The Art of the Paris Chef." *Epicure* (Boston), October 2, 1900.

Audot, Louis Eustache. *La Cuisinière de la Campagne et de la Ville.* Paris: Audot, 1818.

Auslander, Leora. "The Creation of Value and the Production of Good Taste: The Social Life of Furniture in Paris, 1860–1914." Ph.D. dissertation, Brown University, 1988.

———. *Taste and Power: Furnishing Modern France.* Berkeley: University of California Press, 1996.

Barberet, Joseph. *Le Travail en France.* Monographies Professionnelles 6. Paris: Berger-Levrault et Cie, 1889.

Beauvilliers, Antoine. *L'Art du Cuisinier.* Paris: Pilet, 1814.

Bedarida, François. *A Social History of England, 1851–1975.* London: Methuen, 1979.

Blau, Judith. *Architects and Firms: A Sociological Perspective on Architectural Practice*. Cambridge, Mass.: MIT Press, 1984.

Bourdieu, Pierre. *Distinction: A Social Critique of the Judgement of Taste*. Cambridge, Mass.: Harvard University Press, 1984.

Bowlby, Rachel. *Just Looking: Consumer Culture in Dreiser, Gissing, and Zola*. New York: Methuen, 1985.

Braudel, Fernand. *The Structures of Everyday Life*. Vol. 1, *Civilization and Capitalism*. New York: Harper and Row, 1985.

Breckenridge, Carol, and Peter Van der Veer, eds. *Orientalism and the Postcolonial Predicament*. Philadelphia: University of Pennsylvania Press, 1993.

Briggs, Asa. *A Social History of England*. New York: Viking Press, 1983.

Brillat-Savarin, Jean Anthelme. *The Physiology of Taste, Or Meditations on Transcendental Gastronomy*. 1825. Trans. and annotated M. F. K. Fisher. San Francisco: North Point Press, 1986.

Brulon, Dorothée. "Les Services de Porcelaine de Sèvres, Présents des Rois Louis XV et Louis XVI aux Souverains Etrangers." In *Versailles et les Tables Royales en Europe*. Versailles: Réunion des Musées Nationaux, 1993.

Carême, Antonin. 1828. *Le Cuisinier Parisien ou L'Art de la Cuisine Française au Dix-Neuvième Siècle*. Paris: Auteur, 1828.

"Cercle Culinaire et l'Ecole Professionelle de Cuisine." *L'Art Culinaire* 4(23) (December 12, 1886): 261–62.

Chaddock, Gail Russell. "The Precious Few; French Haute Cuisine Is Hanging in There, Barely." *Los Angeles Times*, February 15, 1996, p. 17.

Châtillon-Plessis. "Chronique Professionnelle." *L'Art Culinaire* 8 (12) (June 30, 1890): 125–27.

——. "Chronique Professionelle: Le Cuisinier-Ouvrier." *L'Art Culinaire* 8 (8) (April 30, 1890): 76–79.

——. *La Vie à Table à la Fin du XIXème Siècle: Théorie Pratique et Historique de Gastronomie Moderne*. Paris: Firmin-Dodot, 1894.

Chaucer, Geoffrey. *The Canterbury Tales*. London: Penguin, 1975.

Child, Julia. *Mastering the Art of French Cooking*. Vol. 1. New York: Alfred A. Knopf, 1983.

"Chronique du Jour: A l'Ecole Professionelle de Cuisine." *L'Art Culinaire* 10 (3) (February 15, 1892): 31–32.

Clark, Priscilla. 1975. "Thoughts for Food, I: French Cuisine and French Culture." *French Review* 49 (1) (1975): 32–41.

——. "Thoughts for Food II: Culinary Culture in Contemporary France." *French Review* 49 (2) (1975): 198–205.

Clifford, James. 1992. "Travelling Cultures." In *Cultural Studies*, ed. Lawrence Grossberg and Cary Nelson. London: Routledge, 1992.

Clifford, James, and George E. Marcus, eds. *Writing Culture: The Poetics and Politics of Ethnography*. Berkeley: University of California Press, 1986.

Clough, Shepard Bancroft. *The Economic History of Europe*. Boston: Heath, 1952.

"Club Life." *The Caterer and Household Magazine*, March 1886.

"Clubs of Old and Their Meeting Places." *The Epicure* (London) (December 1903).

Colombié, Auguste. *Traité Pratique de Cuisine Bourgeoise, Suite aux Eléments Culinaires à l'Usage des Jeunes Filles*. Paris: L. Mulo, 1897.

Comaroff, Jean, and John Comaroff. *Of Revelation and Revolution: Christianity, Colonialism, and Consciousness in South Africa*. Chicago: University of Chicago Press, 1991.

"Le Concours Culinaire de Paris." *L'Art Culinaire* 5, (2,3) (January 31, February 7, 1886).

Cosman, Madeleine Pelner. 1976. *Fabulous Feasts: Medieval Cookery and Ceremony*. New York: George Braziller.

"La Crise de l'Apprentissage." *Journal des Confiseurs, Pâtissiers, Glaciers* 20 (1) (January 1909): 1–4.

Crosby, Alfred. *The Columbian Exchange: Biological and Cultural Consequences of 1492*. Westport, Conn.: Greenwood Press, 1972.

La Cuisine d'Aujourd'hui: Ecole des Jeunes Cuisiniers. Paris: Librairie E. Dentu, 1897.

"La Cuisine Française en Angleterre." *L'Art Culinaire* 8(18) (September 1890): iii–ix.

"Les Cuisiniers Français à Londres." *L'Art Culinaire* 8(18) (September 1890): xvi.

"Les Cuisiniers Français en Angleterre." *L'Art Culinaire* (1888): 126–28.

Darnton, Robert. *The Great Cat Massacre and Other Episodes in French History*. New York: Vintage Press, 1984.

David, Elizabeth. *French Country Cooking*. 1951. Reprint, New York: Penguin, 1987.

———. *French Provincial Cooking*. 1960. New York: Penguin, 1983.

Delahaire. *Historique Sommaire de l'Union Philanthropique et de l'Alimentation*. Paris: Archives Nationales.

Deliée, Felix. *The Franco-American Cookery Book*. New York and London: G. P. Putnam's Sons, 1884.

DeSalis, Harriet. *The Art of Cookery Past and Present*. London: Hutchinson, 1898.

Dirks, Nicholas. *The Hollow Crown: Ethnohistory of an Indian Kingdom*. Ann Arbor: University of Michigan Press, 1993.

Distel, Marthe, ed. *La Cuisine Pratique: Démontrée et Raisonnée*. Paris: Cordon Bleu, 1902.

D'Orey, Léonor. "L'Histoire des Services d'Orfèvrerie Française à la Cour du Portugal." In *Versailles et Les Tables Royales en Europe*. Versailles: Réunion des Musées Nationaux, 1993.

Douglas, Mary. *In the Active Voice*. London: Routledge and Kegan Paul, 1982.

Drummond, J. C., and Anne Wilbraham. *The Englishman's Food: Five Centuries of English Diet*. 1939. Reprint London: Pimlico, 1991.

Dubois, Urbain. *Cuisine de Tous les Pays: Etudes Cosmopolites*. Paris: Librairie E. Dentu, 1881.

Dumas, Alexandre. *Dumas on Food*. Trans. Alan Davidson and Jane Davidson. London: Folio Society, 1978.

Dupeux, Georges. *French Society, 1789–1970*. New York: Barnes and Noble, 1976.

Dupré. "Chronique Professionelle." *L'Art Culinaire* 8 (11) (June 15, 1890): 113–14.

Dyer, Christopher. *Standards of Living in the Later Middle Ages: Social Change in England, c. 1200–1520*. Cambridge: Cambridge University Press, 1989.

Edel, Leon. *Henry James: A Life*. New York: Harper and Row, 1985.

"Editorial." *Food and Cookery and the Catering World* (July 29, 1904).

Elias, Norbert. *The Civilizing Process: The History of Manners and Power and Civility*. New York: Pantheon, 1978.

Epstein, Steven A. *Wage Labor and Guilds in Medieval Europe*. Chapel Hill: University of North Carolina Press, 1991.

Escoffier, Auguste. *Auguste Escoffier: Memories of My Life*. New York: Van Nostrand Reinhold, 1997.

———. *The Escoffier Cookbook: A Guide to the Fine Art of French Cuisine*. 1931. Reprint, New York: Crown Publishers, 1969.

———. *Le Guide Culinaire: Aide Mémoire de Cuisine Pratique*. Paris: E. Colin, 1907.

———. *Ma Cuisine, 2500 Recettes*. Paris: Flammarion, 1934.

———. *Souvenirs Inédits*. Paris: Jeanne Laffitte, 1985.

———. "Why Men Make the Best Cooks." Universal Food and Cookery Association, *Annual Report*, 1895, 56–57.

"Evolution in French Cookery." *The Epicure* (London)1 (1903), n.p.

"L'Exposition Culinaire." *Le Pot au Feu* 3(6) (March 15 1895): 77.

"L'Exposition Culinaire Artistique de Londres (1885)." *L'Art Culinaire* 4(1) (January 1886): 10–12.

Favre, Joseph. *Dictionnaire Universel de Cuisine Pratique: Encyclopédie Illustré d'Hygiène Alimentaire*. Paris: Librairie-Imprimerie des Halles et de la Bourse de Commerce, 1894.

Fine, Gary Alan. *Kitchens: The Culture of Restaurant Work*. Berkeley: University of California Press, 1996.

Fink, Beatrice. "A Taste of Diderot." *Oxford Symposium on Food and Cookery: Taste*. London: Prospect Books, 1988.

Fisher, M. F. K. *French Provincial Cooking*. New York: Time-Life Books, 1968.

Flandrin, Jean-Louis. "Distinction Through Taste." In *The History of Private Life*, Vol. 3, ed. Philippe Ariès and Georges Duby. Cambridge, Mass.: Harvard University Press, 1989.

Flandrin, Jean-Louis, and Massimo Montanari. *L'Histoire d'Alimentation*. Paris: Fayard, 1997.

Foucault, Michel. *Power/Knowledge: Selected Interviews and Other Writings*. New York: Pantheon, 1980.

Fox, Richard, ed. *Nationalist Ideologies and the Production of National Cultures*. Washington, D.C.: American Anthropology Association, 1990.

———. *Recapturing Anthropology*. Santa Fe, N.M.: School of American Research Press, 1991.

Francatelli, Charles. *The Modern Cook; A Practical Guide to the Culinary Art in All Its Branches*. 26th edition. London: R. Bentley, 1880.

Franey, Pierre, with Richard Flaste and Bryan Miller. *A Chef's Tale: A Memoir of Food, France and America*. New York: Alfred A. Knopf, 1994.

Franklin, Alfred. *La Vie Privée d'Autrefois: La Cuisine*. 1888. Reprint, Geneva: Editions Slatkine, 1980.

"French and English Cookery Compared." *Caterer and Hotel Proprietor's Gazette* (November 1, 1879): 135–36.

"French Cookery." *Caterer and Hotel Proprietor's Gazette* (March 5, 1881): 37.

Garrett, Theodore Francis. *The Encyclopedia of Practical Cookery*. London: L. Upcott Gill, 1890.

Geertz, Clifford. "Common-Sense as a Cultural System." In *Interpretations of Culture*. New York: Basic Books, 1978.

Gilbert, Philéas. "L'Arbitrage: Ouvriers ou Artistes." *Le Progrès des Cuisiniers* 2(36) (Aug. 1887).

———. "Considérations sur les Apprentis." *L'Art Culinaire* 3(17) (Sept. 1885): 173–75.

———. "La Cuisine et les Cuisiniers." *L'Art Culinaire* 20(11) (June 1, 1902): 42–43.

———. "Des Fonds de Cuisine." *L'Art Culinaire* 3(4) (February 22, 1885): 37–38.

———. "Ecole Professionelle." *Le Progrès des Cuisiniers* 7(140) (April 1, 1892): 1.

Génin, Theodore. "L'Ecole Professionelle de Cuisine." *L'Art Culinaire* 3(14) (July 26, 1885): 141–42.

Gillies, Sarah. 1988. "Reflections in Eighteenth Century Taste." *Oxford Symposium on Food and Cookery: Taste*. London: Prospect Books.

Girouard, Mark. *Victorian Pubs*. New Haven, Conn.: Yale University Press, 1984.

Glasse, Hannah. *The Art of Cookery Made Plain and Easy; which far Exceeds Anything of the Kind ever Published*. 4th edition. London: The Author, 1751.

Goody, Jack. *Cooking, Cuisine, and Class: A Study in Comparative Sociology*. Cambridge: Cambridge University Press, 1982.

Gouffé, Jules. *Le Livre de Cuisine*. Paris: Librairie Hachette, 1902.

Green, Nicholas. *The Spectacle of Nature: Landscape and Bourgeois Culture in Nineteenth-Century France*. Manchester: Manchester University Press, 1990.

Greenhalgh, Paul. *Ephemeral Vistas: The Expositions Universelles, Great Exhibitions, and World's Fairs, 1851–1939*. New York: St. Martin's Press, 1988.

Guérard, Michel. *Cuisine Minceur*. New York: William Morrow, 1976.

Guha, Ranajit. "On Some Aspects of Historiography of Colonial India." In *Subaltern Studies*, ed. Ranajit Guha and Gayatri Spivak. Oxford: Oxford University Press, 1988.

Gupta, Akhil, and James Ferguson. "Beyond 'Culture': Space, Identity, and the Politics of Difference." *Cultural Anthropology* 2 (1) (1992): 6–23.

——. *Culture, Power, and Place: Explorations in Critical Anthropology*. Durham, N.C.: Duke University Press, 1997.

Habermas, Jürgen. "The Public Sphere." In *Rethinking Popular Culture: Contemporary Perspectives in Cultural Studies*, ed. Chandra Mukerji and Michael Schudson. Berkeley: University of California Press, 1991.

Handler, Richard. "High Culture, Hegemony, and Historical Causality." *American Ethnologist*, 19(4) (1992).

Hannerz, Ulf. "Cosmopolitans and Locals in World Culture." *Theory, Culture and Society* 2–3 (June 1990).

Hardin, Kris L. *The Aesthetics of Action: Continuity and Change in a West African Town*. Washington, D.C.: Smithsonian Institution Press, 1993.

Harvey, David. 1989. *Conditions of Postmodernity: An Enquiry into the Origins of Cultural Change*. Oxford: Blackwell, 1989.

Helm, Mary. *Ulysses' Sail: An Ethnographic Odyssey of Power, Knowledge, and Geographical Distance*. Princeton, N.J.: Princeton University Press, 1988.

Henisch, Bridget. *Fast and Feast: Food in Medieval Society*. University Park: Pennsylvania State University Press, 1976.

Herbage, Peter. *A History of the Worshipful Company of Cooks, London*. London: Cook's Guild, 1982.

"Histoire de l'Art Culinaire." *L'Art Culinaire* 10(3) (February 15, 1892): 37–38.

Hobsbawm, Eric J. *The Age of Capital, 1848–1975*. New York: Barnes and Noble, 1975.

——. *The Age of Revolution, 1789–1848*. New York: American Library, 1964.

Hobsbawm, Eric J., and Peter Dimock. *The Age of Empire*. New York: Vintage Press, 1989.

Huetz de Lemps, Alain, and Jean-Robert Pitte. *Les Restaurants dans le Monde et à Travers les Ages*. Grenoble: Editions Glénat, 1990.

Husson, Armand. *Les Consommations de Paris*. 2nd edition. Paris: Librairie Hachette et Cie, 1875.

James, Henry. *Portraits of Places*. New York: Lear Publishers, 1948.

Jerrold, William Blanchard. *The Epicure's Yearbook and Table Companion*. London: Bradbury, Evans, 1868.

Jones, Philip E. *The Butchers of London: A History of the Worshipful Company of Butchers of the City of London*. London: Secker and Warburg, 1976.

Kaplan, Stephen. *Bread, Politics, and Political Economy in the Reign of Louis XV*. The Hague: Martinus Nijhoff, 1976.

———. *Provisioning Paris: Merchants and Millers in the Grain and Flour Trade During the Eighteenth Century*. Ithaca, N.Y.: Cornell University Press, 1984.

Kaplow, Jeffry. *The Names of Kings: The Parisian Laboring Poor in the Eighteenth Century*. New York: Basic Books, 1972.

Karp, Ivan, Christine Mullen Kreamer, and Steven D. Lavine. *Museums and Communities: The Politics of Public Culture*. Washington, D.C.: Smithsonian Institution Press, 1992.

Karp, Ivan, and Steven D. Lavine. *Exhibiting Cultures: The Poetics and Politics of Museum Display*. Washington, D.C.: Smithsonian Institution Press, 1991.

Kingsbury, Henry. *Music, Talent, and Performance: A Conservatory Cultural System*. Philadelphia: Temple University Press, 1988.

Kirwan, A. V. *Host and Guest*. London: Bell and Galdy, 1864.

Larson, Magali Sarfatti. "In the Manner of Experts and Professionals." In *The Formation of Professions: Knowledge, State, and Strategy*, ed. R. Torstendahl and M. Burrage. London: Sage Publications, 1990, 24–50.

———. *The Rise of Professionalism: A Sociological Analysis*. Berkeley: University of California Press, 1977.

Laurioux, Bruno. "Spices in the Medieval Diet: A New Approach." *Food and Foodways* 1 (1985): 43–76.

La Varenne, François-Pierre de. *Le Cuisinier Français: Textes Présentés par Jean-Louis Flandrin, Philip Hyman and Mary Hyman*. La Bibliothèque Blaue. Paris: Montalba, 1983.

Laver, James. *Manners and Morals in the Age of Optimism, 1898–1914*. New York: Harper and Row, 1966.

Lehning, James R. *Peasant and French: Cultural Contact in Rural France During the Nineteenth Century*. Cambridge: Cambridge University Press, 1995.

L'Espinasse, René de. *Les Métiers et Corporations de la Ville de Paris*. Vol 1, *XIV–XVIIIème Siècle, Ordonnances Générales—Métiers d'Alimentation*. Histoire Générale de Paris: Collection des Documents. Paris: Imprimerie Nationale, 1886–87.

Ludden, David. "Orientalist Empiricism: Transformations of Colonial Knowledge." In *Orientalism and the Postcolonial Predicament*, ed. Carol Breckenridge and Peter Van der Veer, editors. Philadelphia: University of Pennsylvania Press, 1993.

Mackenzie, Compton. *The Savoy of London*, London: George G. Harrap, 1953.

Marcus, George, and Michael M. J. Fischer. *Anthropology as Cultural Critique: An Experimental Moment in the Human Sciences*. Chicago: University of Chicago Press, 1986.

Marin, François. *Les Dons de Comus, Ou l'Art de la Cuisine*. 1739. Reprint Paris: Pisot, 1758.

Marx, Karl, and Friedrich Engels. *The Marx-Engels Reader*. Ed. Robert C. Tucker. New York: W. W. Norton, 1978.

Meadab. *Clark's Pocket Paris*. 1900.

Mennell, Stephen. *All Manners of Food: Eating and Taste in England and France from Middle Ages to the Present*. New York: Blackwell, 1985.

Miller, Michael B. *The Bon Marché: Bourgeois Culture and the Department Store, 1869–1920*. Princeton: Princeton University Press, 1981.

Mintz, Sidney. "Cuisine and Haute Cuisine: How Are They Linked?" *Food and Foodways* 3 (3) (1989).

———. *Sweetness and Power: The Place of Sugar in Modern History*. New York: Penguin, 1985.

———. *Tasting Food, Tasting Freedom: Excursions into Eating, Culture, and the Past*. Boston: Beacon Press, 1996.

Monselet, Charles. *Le Double Almanach Gourmand*. Paris: Librairie du Petit Journal, 1866.
———. *Gastronomie, Récits de Table*. Paris: Charpentier, 1874.
Montagné, Prosper. *Larousse Gastronomique*. New York: Crown Publishers, 1961.
Montagné, Prosper, and Prosper Salles. *La Grande Cuisine Illustrée*. Paris: Flammarion, 1929.
Moore, Henrietta L., ed. *The Future of Anthropological Knowledge*. London: Routledge, 1996.
"La Mutualité." *L'Etoile* 1(5) (1874).
Newnham-Davis, Lieut. Col. Nathaniel. *Dinners and Diners: Where and How to Dine in London*. London: Grant Richards, 1899.
———. *The Gourmet Guide to Europe*. London: Grant Richards, 1903.
Nierinck, Edmond, and Jean-Pierre Poulain. *Histoire de la Cuisine et des Cuisiniers: Techniques Culinaires et Pratiques de Table, en France, du Moyen Age à Nos Jours*. Paris: Editions Jacques Lanore, 1992.
Noel-Waldteufel, Marie-France. "Manger à La Cour: Alimentation et Gastronomie aux XVIIème et XVIIIème Siècles." In *Versailles et les Tables Royales en Europe*. Versailles: Réunion des Musées Nationaux, 1993.
Nord, Philip. *Paris Shopkeepers and the Politics of Resentment*. Princeton, N.J.: Princeton University Press, 1986.
Ohnuki-Tierney, Emiko, ed. *Culture Through Time*. Palo Alto, Calif.: Stanford University Press, 1991.
Orwell, George. *Down and Out in Paris and London*. New York: Harvest/HBJ, 1961.
Ousby, Ian. *The Englishman's England: Taste, Travel, and the Rise of Tourism*. Cambridge: Cambridge University Press, 1990.
Ozanne, Achille. "Deux Jours à Londres." *L'Art Culinaire* 5(10) (May 31, 1887).
———. 1887. "La Revue de Concours: Les Apprentis et Retour au Buffet." *L'Art Culinaire* 5(1) (January 1887): 91–94.
Pellaprat, Henri. *Le Cuisinier*. Paris: Berger-Levrault, 1942.
Pépin, Jacques. *La Technique*. New York: Pocket Books, 1976.
Perkin, Harold. *The Rise of Professional Society: England Since 1880*. London: Routledge, 1989.
"Placement Gratuit des Ouvriers Pâtissiers-Cuisiniers." *Le Progrès Gastronomique* 1(2) (1884): 1–4.
"Portraits of Great Chefs." *Cook's Journal* (1882): 10.
"Le Progrès de la Chambre Syndicale des Cuisiniers de Paris." *Le Progrès des Cuisiniers* 1(1) (1886).
"Protestation." *Le Progrès des Cuisiniers* 6(1), January 1891.
Rabinow, Paul. *French Modern: Norms and Forms in the Social Environment*. Cambridge, Mass.: MIT Press, 1989.
Reader, W. J. *Professional Men: The Rise of the Professional Classes in Nineteenth-Century England*. London: Weidenfeld and Nicolson, 1966.
"Réglements." *L'Art Culinaire* 9(1) (January 15, 1891): 4–5.
"Les Restaurants Anglais." *L'Art Culinaire* (September 1890): xii–xvi.
Revel, Jean-François. *Culture and Cuisine: A Journey Through the History of Food*. New York: DaCapo Press, 1982.
Ritz, Marie. *César Ritz, Host to the World*. Philadelphia: J. B. Lippincott, 1938.
Rogers, Susan Carol. *Shaping Modern Times in Rural France: The Transformation and Reproduction of an Aveyronnais Community*. Princeton, N.J.: Princeton University Press, 1991.
"Rome Gourmande." *L'Art Culinaire* 20(23) (December 1, 1902): iv–xxii.
Root, Waverly. *The Food of France*. 1958. Reprint New York: Vintage, 1977.

Rosenzweig, Roy. "The Rise of the Saloon." In *Rethinking Popular Culture: Contemporary Perspectives in Cultural Studies*, ed. Chandra Mukerji and Michael Schudson. Berkeley: University of California Press, 1991.

Said, Edward. *Culture and Imperialism*. New York: Alfred A. Knopf, 1993.

———. *Orientalism*. New York: Vintage Books, 1978.

Saint-Ange, Madame. *La Cuisine de Madame Saint-Ange*. Grenoble: Editions Choix, 1957.

Saulniers, Louis. *Le Répertoire de la Cuisine*. Paris, 1914.

Scully, Terence, ed. *The Viandier of Taillevent: An Edition of All Extant Manuscripts*. Ottawa: University of Ottawa Press, 1988.

Senn, C. Hermann. *The Souvenir of the Cookery Annual*. To Commemorate the Coming of Age of the Universal Food and Cookery Association. London: Food and Cookery Publishing Agency, 1907.

Silverman, Deborah L. *Art Nouveau in Fin-de-Siècle France: Politics, Psychology, and Style*. Berkeley: University of California Press, 1989.

Simon, André. *A Concise Encyclopedia of Gastronomy*. London: Collins, 1952.

Simon, Jules. *L'Ecole*. Paris: Librairie Internationale, 1865.

Sonnenfeld, Albert. "The Chef as Hero: Microwaves in the Sea of Culinary History." *Journal of Gastronomy* 3 (2) (1986): 27–39.

Soyer, Alexis. *Memoirs of Alexis Soyer*. Ed. F. Volant and J. R. Warren. Rottingdean, Sussex : Cooks Books, 1985.

Spang, Rebecca. "A Confusion of Appetites: The Emergence of Paris Restaurant Culture, 1740–1848." Dissertation, Cornell University, 1993.

Stouff, Louis. *Ravitaillement et Alimentation en Provence aux 14ème et 15ème Siècles*. Paris: Mouton., 1970.

Strong, Rowland. *Where and How to Dine in Paris*. London: G. Richards, 1900.

Suleri, Sara. *The Rhetoric of British India*. Chicago: University of Chicago Press, 1992.

Sussman, Warren. *Culture as History: The Transformation of American Society in the Twentieth Century*. New York: Pantheon, 1984.

Terrio, Susan. 1996. "Crafting *Grand Cru* Chocolates in Contemporary France." *American Anthropologist* 98 (1) (March 1996): 65–80.

Thomas, Dana. "Sushi Cordon Bleu? Foreign Foods Invade the Land of Haute Cuisine." *Newsweek* 127 (3) (1996): 41.

Thrupp, Sylvia. *A Short History of the Worshipful Company of Bakers of London*. London: Company of Bakers, 1933.

Toomre, Joyce. *Classic Russian Cooking: Elena Molokhovets' A Gift to Young Housewives*. Bloomington: Indiana University Press, 1992.

"Tout Est dans Tout." *La Cuisine Française et Etrangère* 98(9) (September 1889): 135–36.

"The Trade Section." *Food and Cookery and the Catering World* (1904).

Tschumi, Gabriel. "Mémoires." In *Annals of Labour: Autobiographies of Working Class People, 1820–1920*, ed. John Burnett. Bloomington: Indiana University Press, 1974. 193–203.

Turner, Bryan S. 1985. "Review Article, *The Court Society* and *The Civilizing Process*, vol. 2, *Power and Civility*." *Theory, Culture, and Society* 2(3) (1985): 158–61.

Universal Food and Cookery Association. *Annual Report*. 1895.

Virmaître, Charles. "Un Ecole pour Cuisiniers à Londres." *L'Etoile* 1(17) (1874).

Wallerstein, Immanuel, and Roy Boyne. "Culture as the Ideological Battleground of the Marxian World System." *Theory, Culture, and Society* 2(3) (June 1990): 31–55, 1990.

Walton, Whitney. *France at the Crystal Palace: Bourgeois Taste and Artisan Manufacture in the Nineteenth Century*. Berkeley: University of California Press, 1992.

Weber, Eugen. *Peasants into Frenchmen: The Modernization of Rural France, 1870–1914*. Stanford, Calif.: Stanford University Press, 1976.

Weiss, John H. "Bridges and Barriers: Narrowing Access and Changing Structure in the French Engineering Profession, 1800–1850." In *Professions and the French State, 1700–1900*, ed. Gerald L. Geison. Philadelphia: University of Pennsylvania Press, 1984.

Wells, Patricia, and Joel Rubochon. *Simply French*. New York: William Morrow, 1991.

Wheaton, Barbara Ketcham. *Savoring The Past: The French Kitchen and Table from 1300 to 1789*. Philadelphia: University of Pennsylvania Press, 1983.

Whitton, Joseph. 1886. "The Clubbable Man." *The Caterer and Household Magazine* (March 1886).

Willan, Anne. *Great Cooks and Their Recipes: From Taillevent to Escoffier*, London: Elm Tree Books, 1977.

Williams, Raymond. *The Country and the City*. New York: Oxford University Press, 1973.

———. *Keywords: A Vocabulary of Culture and Society*. New York: Oxford University Press, 1985.

Williams, Rosalind. "The Dream World of Mass Consumption." In *Rethinking Popular Culture: Contemporary Perspectives in Cultural Studies*, ed. Chandra Mukerji and Michael Schudson. Berkeley: University of California Press, 1991.

Willis, Paul. *Learning to Labor: How Working Class Kids Get Working Class Jobs*. New York: Columbia University Press, 1977.

Wilson, C. Anne. "Ritual, Form and Colour in the Mediaeval Food Tradition." In *The Appetite and The Eye: Visual Aspects of Food and Its Presentation Within Their Historic Context*. Edinburgh: Edinburgh University Press, 1991.

Wolf, Eric. *Europe and the People Without History*. Berkeley: University of California Press, 1982.

Woodbridge, George. *The Reform Club, 1836–1976: A History from the Club's Records*. London: Published by Members of the Reform Club in Association with Clearwater Publishing Company, New York, 1978.

Yates, Lucy H. 1906. "Review of the 17th Universal Food and Cookery Exhibition." *The Epicure* (London) (December 1906).

Zeldin, Theodore. *France 1848–1945: Taste and Corruption*. Oxford: Oxford University Press, 1980.

———. *France 1848–1945: Intellect and Pride*. Oxford: Oxford University Press, 1980.

ACKNOWLEDGMENTS

I happily acknowledge the contribution of colleagues, friends, and family to this book. Arjun Appadurai, Kris Hardin, Rebecca Huss-Ashmore, and David Ludden supported my wish to research and write on an unconventional topic, and I benefited enormously from their advice, ideas, and encouragement. As my adviser, Arjun encouraged and protected me as I journeyed far into the land of French haute cuisine. A special note of thanks goes to David Ludden, whose intellectual commitment and friendship gave me the courage to carry out the project. At a very crucial juncture he read the manuscript and provided valuable insights and suggestions.

For their gracious hospitality and companionship, my appreciation goes to Bing Broderick, Ellen Brodsky, Nick DeGenova, Carrick Eggleston, Phil Esocoff, Karen Floreen, Amy Friedman, Laura Hostetler, Penny M. Hunt, Ritty Lukose, Ted Rybeck, Sarah Strauss, Rosemary Van Allan, and Amy Weinstein. Beebe Bahrani, Carolyn Behrman, Sanjay Joshi, Mark Liechty, and Rachel Tolen read various chapters along the way, and their comments did much to help clarify my ideas. John Feffer read the revised manuscript and provided valuable advice on organization as well as plenty of encouragement. André Burnier allowed me to use his personal collection of nineteenth-century French cookbooks, for which I am extremely grateful.

Deb Dwyer edited the entire manuscript with care; her stylistic advice was a gift during the initial revision process. My colleagues and students at the New England Culinary Institute have listened patiently to my stories of France, chefs, and haute cuisine, while the administration was responsive to my often unusual requests for time to finish the project. Special thanks go to Cynthia Belliveau, Kerry Litchfield, and Ellen McShane. At the final hour, Cybil Brown, Aubrey de Gray, Genevieve Ehlers, Joshua Grinker, and Ritty Lukose stepped in with important technical support.

My research trips to Europe were funded by two grants: the Julia Child Research Fellowship from the International Association of Culinary Professionals and the Penfield Fellowship in Diplomacy and Belles Lettres from the University of Pennsylvania. The New England Culinary Institute granted me a sabbatical that allowed me to do important final revisions.

I did library research at the Bibliothèque Nationale; Archives Nationales; Bibliothèque de la Ville de Paris; British Museum Library; Guildhall Library; Archives of the Westminster Technical College; Library of Congress; Schlesinger Library at Radcliffe College; Library Company of Philadelphia; Center of Research Holdings; and the John Crerar Library at the University of Chicago. The highlight of this research was my time spent at the Schlesinger Library. Barbara Haber, curator of books, was an amazing resource and guide. I also had the tremendous pleasure of working with Barbara Ketcham Wheaton, the curator of the Culinary Collection. Her erudition and dedication to the field of culinary history have been an inspiration to me. Barbara Wheaton also graciously read the entire manuscript twice. Her unerring eye for historical detail and her insistence on clear language made this a much better book. During the ethnographic portion of my research, Lesley Gray and Susan Epstein at the Cordon Bleu Cookery School in London were especially generous with their time.

Patricia Smith at the University of Pennsylvania Press has been a tireless champion of this project. Noreen O'Connor, Alison Johnson, Alison Anderson, and Bruce Franklin have been wonderful guides as well.

It is not enough simply to acknowledge my family, but for now a "thank you" must suffice. Involved in their own intellectual endeavors, David Trubek, Louise Trubek, Jessica Trubek, Jeffrey Pence, and Anne Trubek all graciously supported mine. Bradley Koehler deserves a round of applause and a glass of champagne. Both as husband and as chef he has been a true source of support, comfort, knowledge, and inspiration. Thanks for being so patient.

INDEX